International
and U.S. IPO
Planning

Other Works by Frederick D. Lipman

Executive Compensation Best Practices

Corporate Governance Best Practices: Strategies for Public, Private, and Not-for-Profit Organizations

Valuing Your Business: Strategies to Maximize the Sale Price

Audit Committees

The Complete Guide to Employee Stock Options

The Complete Guide to Valuing and Selling Your Business

The Complete Going Public Handbook

Financing Your Business with Venture Capital

How Much Is Your Business Worth

Going Public

Venture Capital and Junk Bond Financing

INTERNATIONAL AND U.S. IPO PLANNING

A Business Strategy Guide

FREDERICK D. LIPMAN

WILEY

John Wiley & Sons, Inc.

Library of Congress Cataloging-in-Publication Data

Lipman, Frederick D.
  International and US IPO planning : a business strategy guide /
Frederick D. Lipman.
       p. cm.
  Includes index.
  ISBN 978-0-470-39087-0 (cloth)
  1. Going public (Securities)–United States. 2. Corporations–United States–Finance. 3. Going public (Securities) 4. Corporations–Finance.
I. Title.
  HG4028.S7L57 2009
  658.15'224–dc22   2008029057

Printed in the United States of America

10 9 8 7 6 5 4 3 2 1

To my partners at Blank Rome LLP, who gave me the time to write this book

Contents

PART THREE

TRADITIONAL AND NONTRADITIONAL
IPOS IN THE UNITED STATES   163

Acknowledgments

The author wishes to acknowledge the assistance of the following attorneys at Blank Rome LLP and its Hong Kong subsidiary in preparing this book: Yelena M. Barychev, Esq., Nigel J. Binnersley, a Hong Kong solicitor, Tim Drew, a Hong Kong solicitor, Joseph T. Gulant, Esq., Raanan Persky, an Israeli attorney and a foreign legal consultant in Pennsylvania, Brad L. Shiffman, Esq., Jane K. Storero, Esq., Jeffrey M. Taylor, Esq., and Ted Tang, a Hong Kong trainee solicitor. Ann Margrete Ringheim, a Norwegian attorney, also was helpful in preparing the appendices to this book. I want to express my special appreciation to Jane K. Storero, Esq., who spent time reviewing the entire book.

Some of the chapters of this book were authored or co-authored by others. Jeffrey M. Taylor, Esq., a securities lawyer with expertise on international IPOs, co-authored the "Avoiding SOX" section of Chapter 9. Tim Drew, a solicitor and notary in the Hong Kong office of Blank Rome LLP, co-authored the description of Hong Kong Stock Exchange contained in Chapter 9. Joseph T Gulant, Esq., an international tax expert, authored Chapter 10. Jane Storero, Esq., a securities lawyer with expertise on public shells, authored Chapter 12. Brad L. Shiffman, Esq., a securities lawyer with expertise on SPACs, authored Chapter 13.

The author also acknowledges the outstanding services of Barbara Helverson, who served as an editor as well as the typist for this book.

Introduction

Going public is the dream of many private companies, regardless of where in the world they are located. Founders of private companies can maintain their control positions in the public company and still sell their personal stock to diversify their investments. Public companies typically can raise capital more cheaply and easily than private companies, with far fewer operational restrictions. Much of the wealth of the Fortune 300 families resulted from their association with founders of public companies.

Although excessive U.S. regulation has sullied the initial public offering (IPO) dream of many smaller U.S. private companies, international IPO markets are still available and increasingly hospitable to IPOs of private companies located throughout the world. The Alternative Investment Market (AIM) of the London Stock Exchange, discussed in Chapter 9 of this book, has proven attractive to smaller private companies around the world, including smaller U.S. companies.

In an increasingly "flat" world,[1] private companies must consider global opportunities for IPOs in those countries with the highest valuation potential and the most hospitable regulatory environment. Although the U.S. markets are still very competitive on the valuation of private companies, they are not necessarily competitive in the regulatory environment, particularly for smaller public companies. Traditional U.S. IPOs with bulge bracket underwriters require post-IPO valuations substantially exceeding $100 million, and preferably at least $250 million, in order to be of interest to institutional investors and to be followed by securities analysts. Therefore, smaller private companies wishing to have a U.S. IPO must either use lower-tier underwriters or be merged into a public shell (Chapter 12) or a special-purpose acquisition company (SPAC, discussed in Chapter 13).

Warren Buffett has stated in his famous letter contained in the Berkshire-Hathaway 2007 annual report:

Despite our country's many imperfections and unrelenting problems of one sort or another, America's rule of law, market-responsive economic system, and belief in meritocracy are almost certain to produce ever-growing prosperity for its citizens.

Although this may be true, other countries are developing a similar culture and in the future may be equally attractive.

In Chapter 1 we explore the pros and cons of a U.S. IPO, including why the U.S. IPO market has become less hospitable for IPOs of smaller private companies and what can be done to make the United States more internationally competitive. Although the country is very competitive in valuing IPOs, its regulatory structure is burdensome, particularly for smaller companies, compared to international alternatives, which are discussed in Chapter 9.

In Part One of this book (Chapters 2 through 8), we discuss advance planning techniques for both an international and a U.S. IPO, with the primary emphasis on U.S. IPOs.

Chapter 2 covers the necessity of developing an impressive management team and how to use equity incentives to attract and retain key executives. One-man or one-woman companies are not good IPO candidates. Underwriters want to see IPO candidates who use a team approach to management.

Chapter 3 discusses methods of growing the business to make the company attractive for an IPO. We note that future growth potential is the most important ingredient of an attractive IPO candidate and give examples of IPOs by companies with little or no revenue but great growth potential. Chapter 3 also discusses acquisitions and so-called *roll-ups* to increase the size of the company prior to an IPO.

Chapter 4 examines the necessity of having auditing or auditable financial statements, the lack of which will prevent an IPO. This chapter also covers the problem of when companies can recognize revenue for accounting purposes, which is a hot-button issue with the Securities and Exchange Commission (SEC) and has hindered many U.S. IPOs.

Chapter 5 discusses the necessity of changing business practices that may violate law well before an IPO, since these questionable business practices can prevent an IPO. We also examine in detail the increasing enforcement activities against violations of the U.S. Foreign Corrupt Practices Act and similar laws in other countries.

Chapter 6 reviews the defenses to a potential hostile takeover of the company that should be in place prior to an IPO. We give examples of provisions that can be inserted into the charter of the public company to deter unwanted suitors, including hedge funds and other activist shareholders.

Chapter 7 discusses the corporate governance mechanisms that should be in place well before an IPO target date, including the formation of an audit committee consisting of independent directors, the development of good internal controls, and a whistleblower policy.

Chapter 8 covers two topics of importance in IPO planning. First, we discuss the possibility of creating insider bailout opportunities before the IPO so that some of the proceeds from the IPO can be directly or indirectly received by insiders. Second, we discuss the necessity of taking advantage of IPO windows, including IPOs in the same industry or certain IPO fads that occur from time to time.

Part Two of this book (Chapters 9 and 10) covers international IPOs. In Chapter 9 we discuss the methodology of structuring an IPO for a U.S. company. We review the mechanics of forming a foreign holding company and avoiding the burdensome reporting requirements of SEC rules as well as costly provisions of the Sarbanes-Oxley Act of 2002 (SOX). We also explore in detail in this chapter an AIM public offering as well as public offerings on other international stock markets, such as the Growth Enterprise Market (GEM) of the Hong Kong Stock Exchange. Chapter 9 also contains a comparison of the costs of an IPO on Nasdaq and on the AIM and a comparison of post-IPO costs on both exchanges.

Chapter 10 deals with the U.S. federal income taxes of international IPOs by U.S. companies and therefore complements Chapter 9.

Part Three of this book (Chapters 11 through 15) describes both traditional and nontraditional IPOs in the United States.

In Chapter 11 we describe in detail the typical IPO process in the United States, with an example of an underwritten public offering and the costs of doing so.

In Chapters 12 through 15 we discuss alternatives to the traditional U.S. IPO that may be of interest to small businesses. Chapter 12 covers reverse mergers into public shells, which is an alternative (albeit risky) for smaller private companies that wish to become part of a publicly held company.

Chapter 13 deals with the very recent phenomenon of forming publicly traded special-purpose acquisition companies (SPACS) with significant capital and having the private company merge into the SPAC.

Chapter 14 deals with Regulation A offerings, which permit private companies to raise up to $5 million over a 12-month period. Chapter 15 covers the so-called SCOR (small corporate offering registration) offering, which permits private companies to raise up to $1 million over a 12-month period.

Appendix A of this book contains a list of the international stock exchange Web sites that can supply valuable listing information to those companies considering an international IPO. Appendix B contains selected responses we received from a survey we conducted of the international stock exchanges.

NOTES

1. Thomas Friedman, *The World Is Flat* (New York: Penguin Books, 2006).

International and U.S. IPO Planning

Chapter 1

Pros and Cons of a U.S. IPO

The New York Stock Exchange (NYSE) and the Nasdaq Stock Market (Nasdaq) are the most prestigious stock markets in the world and are likely to remain so for the next five years. However, they are facing increasing competition from foreign stock exchanges.

A private company considering an initial public offering (IPO), regardless of where in the world the private company is located, should first consider the NYSE and the Nasdaq for an IPO because these stock markets are well regulated and highly liquid and have strong corporate governance standards. For private companies that will have, after an IPO, a market valuation of over $250 million, these prestigious U.S. exchanges are the first places to consider. However, this is not necessarily true for smaller private companies (whether U.S. or international) planning an IPO, as discussed later in this chapter.

We begin the discussion of the pros and cons of a U.S. IPO by considering two topics:

1. Underwriter spreads and underpricing
2. IPO offering expenses and post-IPO compliance expenses

We then review the increasing international competition with U.S. IPO markets, particularly for smaller IPOs, and the reasons why smaller companies may wish to consider an international IPO as an alternative. Finally, we suggest changes that can be made to the U.S. regulatory structure to make it more attractive for smaller IPOs.

UNDERWRITER SPREADS AND UNDERPRICING

Underwriter spreads,[1] or "discounts," in the traditional U.S. IPO market typically run approximately 7%. Strong IPOs may have underwriter discounts less than 7%; weak IPOs may have underwriter discounts higher than 7%. The term "underwriter discount" refers to the excess of the IPO public offering price for the stock that is sold by the underwriter to the public over the price paid to the company for that stock by the underwriter. For example, if the IPO public offering price is $20 per share, and the price that the underwriter pays to the company is $18.60, the $1.40 difference is the 7% underwriter discount.

In contrast, it has been reported that underwriter discounts in a number of foreign IPO offerings are as low as 2%. (See Exhibit 1.1 on international underwriter spreads; although somewhat dated, it is still relevant.) Although this is a major cost differential, particularly in a large offering, it can be justified in some cases by the higher valuation for the company obtained in the U.S. market and the better distribution of the shares sold in the IPO. Likewise, if the U.S. underwriter provides greater after-market support for the stock, this could also justify the greater underwriter discount.

One study in 2002 found that although foreign issuers pay more to get a U.S. lead bank to arrange a bookbuilding IPO, they also end up with lower underpricing. (Underpricing is the percentage difference between the price at which the IPO shares were sold to investors—the public offering price—and the price at which the shares subsequently trade in the market.) The higher U.S. underwriter discount is generally more than offset by savings in the underpricing, which is the amount of money left on the table by the IPO company.[2] A 2004 study found

Exhibit 1.1 Spread Levels in IPO Markets around the World Based upon 10,990 IPOs

	Mode Spread		Gross Spread (%)
Countries	Level (%)	Relative Frequency	Median
Australia	4.00	21.2%	4.0
Hong Kong	2.50	94.8%	2.5
India	2.50	86.0%	2.5
Indonesia	3.50	27.3%	3.5
Malaysia	2.00	88.8%	2.0
New Zealand	nm	nm	5.5
Philippines	3.00	65.4%	5.5
Singapore	2.50	55.7%	2.5
Thailand	3.00	42.9%	3.0
Total Asia Pacific	**2.50**	**66.7%**	**2.5**
Austria	3.00	18.5%	3.5
Belgium	2.50	66.7%	2.5
Denmark	4.00	25.0%	4.0
Finland	4.00	25.0%	3.8
France	3.00	34.0%	3.0
Germany	4.00	38.6%	4.0
Greece	3.00	40.0%	3.0
Ireland	nm	nm	3.3
Italy	4.00	18.2%	4.0
Netherlands	3.25	13.0%	3.7
Norway	4.00	28.6%	4.1
Portugal	3.25	16.7%	3.5
Spain	3.50	26.5%	3.5
Sweden	4.50	14.8%	4.3
Switzerland	4.00	33.3%	4.0
United Kingdom	6.00	8.9%	3.6
Total Europe	**4.00**	**15.6%**	**4.0**
Canada	6.00	18.3%	6.5
United States	7.00	43.0%	7.0
Total North America	**7.00**	**39.8%**	**7.0**

Source: Journal of Financial and Quantitative Analysis, Vol. 38, No. 3, pp. 475–501 (September 2003); Social Science Research Network, www.ssrn.com/.

that underpricing is reduced by 41.6% on average when U.S. banks and U.S. investors are involved. Even after the higher underwriter discount charged by U.S. underwriters is subtracted, one study estimated that 73% of issuers would have been worse off had they chosen foreign banks and foreign investors.[3] However, it is not clear that the U.S. IPO has any significant underpricing advantage when compared to an IPO on the Alternative Investment Market (AIM) of the London Stock Exchange, as discussed in Chapter 9.

An interesting study of U.S. IPOs found that the higher the selling concession made by the underwriter to the selling group of investment bankers, the higher the IPO offering price and consequently the lower the underpricing. This study suggests that IPO candidates should be looking for underwriters that provide generous selling concessions to the selling group.[4]

Underpricing varies from country to country and is markedly lower in some countries, such as Denmark, Luxembourg and certain South American countries,[5] and is markedly higher in China. The average underpricing of Chinese IPOs is 247%, the highest of any major world market.[6]

IPO OFFERING EXPENSES AND POST-IPO COMPLIANCE EXPENSES

IPOs in the United States typically have significantly higher offering expenses than international IPOs. Legal and accounting fees, printing, and other related expenses are substantially higher in the United States than in many other countries. Chapter 9 contains a 2006 comparison of IPO offering expenses on AIM versus a Nasdaq IPO that indicates that the Nasdaq IPO expenses are more than $1.8 million higher than the AIM IPO expenses.[7] However, the legal and accounting expenses quoted in 2007 for AIM offerings are, as a result of the devaluation of the U.S. dollar, in the neighborhood of $400,000 to $1 million each and therefore do not significantly differ from U.S. legal and accounting expenses.[8]

The Tel Aviv Stock Exchange claims that the legal, accounting, printing, and public relations costs for its IPOs are only $155,000 and annual maintenance costs (excluding directors' and officers' [D & O] insurance) are only $260,000.[9] IPO expenses on the Bombay Stock Exchange in India are estimated to be 65% to 75% lower than U.S. costs.[10]

Except for small public offerings, offering expenses are only a very small percentage of the net proceeds of most IPOs. The tendency for U.S. IPOs to be less "underpriced" than international IPOs may make up for all or some of the difference in these offering expenses. However, the advocates for AIM IPOs dispute the assertion that their IPOs have any greater underpricing than U.S. IPOs (see Chapter 9).

The post-IPO regulatory compliance expenses are also significantly higher in the United States than internationally. These post-IPO compliance expenses are usually not material for large-capitalization (cap) IPOs. For companies having a post-IPO market value of less than $250 million, these expenses can be material. These expenses can become very material for companies having a post-IPO market value of less than $100 million. For example, it has been estimated that, annually, the cost of being a $200 million market cap public company on Nasdaq is more than $1.4 million higher than the annual cost of an AIM public company.[11]

INCREASING COMPETITION TO U.S. IPO MARKETS

The competitiveness of the U.S. public market has been seriously challenged in recent years.[12] For example, during the dot-com boom the European IPO market attracted more IPOs in the years 1998 to 2000 than the U.S. stock markets.[13]

According to a report by the Committee on Capital Markets Regulation, the competitiveness of the U.S. public markets has deteriorated significantly in recent years.[14] The report states:

Whereas 43 foreign companies cross-listed in the U.S. without raising capital in 2000, only 4 did so in 2007 through September. In 2006, six foreign companies cross-listed in the U.S. The obvious inference is that foreign companies see diminishing value in bonding to U.S. standards.

In addition, through October 2007, a record of 56 foreign companies delisted from the NYSE.

According to the report, in 1996, 8 of 20 of the largest global IPOs were in the United States, whereas none of the 20 largest global IPOs was conducted in the United States in 2007. IPOs of U.S. companies abroad increased from 0.1% during the 1996 through 2005 period to 4.3% in 2007.

One can argue that the growth of economies outside of the United States is a significant contributor to the growing international IPO competition. However, that is not the only reason. The Sarbanes-Oxley Act of 2002 (SOX) has given the U.S. markets a bad international reputation.

One commentator has stated:

> The now-infamous Sarbanes-Oxley Act in the United States . . . created massive barriers to fraud but, in its wake, a negative environment for the US exchanges. The cost for issuers of compliance with Sarbanes-Oxley reached such a high level that those with a choice started to abandon US equity markets.[15]

The poor reputation of SOX internationally is mostly undeserved, with one major exception and several minor ones. The major exception is the provision of Section 404 that required an auditor attestation report on internal controls. That provision initially caused major cost expenditures by public companies, primarily as a result of poor regulatory implementation (which has now, it is hoped, been corrected), but unfortunately seriously damaged the international reputation of SOX. Some U.S. audit committee chairpersons currently believe that Section 404 of SOX actually has been of significant benefit to their companies by forcing the improvement of internal controls.

According to the report of the Committee on Capital Markets Regulation, as illustrated in Exhibit 1.2,[16] through the third quarter of 2007,

Exhibit 1.2 Share of Global IPOs (Narrowly Defined) Captured by U.S. Exchange

	1996	1997	1998	1999	2000	2001	2002	2003	2004	2005	2006	2007*
Total Number of Global IPOs	105	118	85	112	136	45	47	54	122	192	237	209
Number of Global IPOs Listed on a U.S. Exchange	61	57	41	52	74	10	3	5	28	28	34	32
% of Total Number	55.8%	48.3%	48.2%	46.4%	54.4%	22.2%	6.4%	9.3%	23.0%	14.6%	14.3%	15.3%
($ billions)												
Total Value of Global IPOs	32.3	46.8	25.2	45.4	43.1	15.1	3.7	12.4	21.5	40.5	97.8	
Value of Global IPOs Listed on a U.S. Exchange	24.9	34.3	15.6	34.4	35.3	7.6	2.5	4.9	9.2	4.5	10.8	8.5
% of Total Value	77.3%	73.3%	62.0%	75.8%	81.8%	50.6%	67.1%	39.5%	42.7%	11.2%	11.0%	13.8%

*2007 data through September.

Source: Dealogic.

NOTE: According to Renaissance Capital (www.ipohome.com), Visa's record $17.9 billion U.S. IPO in March 2008 helped the U.S. increase its total IPO proceeds to 33% during the first six months of 2008; however, excluding Visa, the remaining 16 U.S. IPOs captured just 7% of global IPO proceeds during this period.

15.3% of global IPOs were listed on a U.S. exchange, compared with
an average of 51.1% in the period from 1996 to 2000. Similarly, U.S.
exchanges have captured just 13.8% of the total value of global IPOs
to date in 2007, compared with an average of 74.0% in the period
from 1996 to 2000.

The report of the Committee on Capital Markets Regulation goes
on to discuss the increasing trend of U.S. companies listing their IPOs
only on a foreign exchange, as illustrated in Exhibit 1.3.[17]

The only positive trend reflected in the report of the Committee on
Capital Markets Regulation is the increase in the value of "Rule 144A
IPOs," which is defined as IPOs by foreign companies *privately* offered in the United States pursuant to Securities and Exchange Com-
mission(SEC) Rule 144A. As noted in the report:

> ... the Rule 144A market is not subject to SEC regulation under the
> '34 Act (including the Sarbanes-Oxley Act) and the standard of liabili-
> ty is lower than in the public market . Moreover, because access to this
> market is restricted to large institutions, the risk of securities class ac-
> tions is generally lower.

In effect, the foreign companies are willing to raise capital in the
United States only if they are exempted from SEC reporting requirements and SOX.

The report of the Committee on Capital Markets Regulation is further
supported by statistics from the World Federation of Exchanges.[18]
Exhibit 1.4 is an excerpt from a chart in the annual report of the World
Federation of Exchanges on the number of newly listed companies by
each exchange. The chart reflects the growing importance of the London Stock Exchange, Shanghai Stock Exchange, and the Hong Kong
Exchanges. Because these figures include IPOs and listings of investment funds, they significantly overstate the actual dollar amount of
IPOs of operating companies, particularly for the NYSE.

Some have argued that the decline in the IPO market share of U.S.
securities exchanges is due to the greater number of capital choices
available to U.S. private companies. It is true that a foreign private

Exhibit 1.3 Share of U.S. IPOs Listed Only on Foreign Exchanges

	1996	1997	1998	1999	2000	2001	2002	2003	2004	2005	2006	2007*
Total Number of U.S.-Domiciled IPOs	497	398	300	459	341	119	157	129	263	232	189	163
Number of U.S.-Domiciled IPOs Listed Abroad Only	1	0	2	0	0	0	2	1	5	8	12	15
% of Total Number	0.2%	0.0%	0.7%	0.0%	0.0%	0.0%	1.3%	0.8%	1.9%	3.4%	6.3%	9.2%
($ billions)												
Total Value of U.S.-Domiciled IPOs	28.0	32.5	37.5	65.7	62.6	45.2	41.7	44.7	65.9	55.1	44.2	57.4
Value of U.S.-Domiciled IPOs Listed Abroad Only	0.0	0.0	0.0	0.0	0.0	0.0	0.0	0.0	0.1	0.5	0.5	2.5
% of Total Value	0.0%	0.0%	0.0%	0.0%	0.0%	0.0%	0.0%	0.1%	0.2%	0.9%	1.1%	4.3%

*2007 data through September.

Source: Dealogic.

company wishing to raise capital in its home country may be forced into an IPO solely because of the lack of local private equity resources. However, an equally plausible explanation is that there is no easily accessible IPO market in the United States for smaller companies and that the costs and burdens of a U.S. IPO substantially exceed those of any other country. Thus, small U.S. private companies wishing to obtain growth capital are forced to seek private equity financing.

Private equity is not necessarily the best alternative to grow a private company. By their nature, private equity funds will tend to place lower valuations on their investee companies than the IPO marketplace, may have shorter exit horizons and different objectives from the founders of these investee companies, and may take control of the private company away from the founders, leveraging the company with significant debt. The presence of a strong IPO market permits founders and other entrepreneurs to retain control of the public company after the IPO, and to grow the company with less dilutive public equity. More important, an active IPO market serves a social purpose by permitting the public, including persons who could not qualify to invest in private equity funds, to invest in new growth companies.

Exhibit 1.4 Exchange Listings

| | | | Newly Listed Companies 2007 | |
| | (US$ millions) Initial Public | | Domestic | Foreign |
Exchange	Offering	Total	Companies	Companies
Americas				
American SE	N/A	92	71	21
Bermuda SE	N/A	6	0	6
Buenos Aires SE	234.1	5	5	0
Colombia SE	4,597.1	7	7	0
Lima SE	0.0	15	8	7
Mexican Exchange	888.0	63	4	59
Nasdaq	16,192.6	153	128	25
NYSE Group	60,385.8	126	84	42
Santiago SE	230.2	6	4	2

São Paulo SE	27,834.2	70	64	6
TSX Group	7,369.5	408	381	27
Asia Pacific				
Australian SE	16,725.5	292	276	16
Bombay SE	9,642.8	136	136	0
Bursa Malaysia	317.4	22	22	0
Columbo SE	0.0	0	0	0
Hong Kong Exchanges	37,485.9	84	82	2
Indonesia SE	1,976.3	22	22	0
Jasaq	688.6	49	49	0
Korea Exchange	3,170.0	98	96	2
National Stock Exchange India	7,874.1	201	201	0
New Zealand Exchange	316.7	9	7	2
Osaka SE	179.5	28	28	0
Philippine SE	412.1	11	11	0
Shanghai SE	57,770.0	25	25	0
Shenzhen SE	5,670.7	101	101	0
Singapore Exchange	5,159.8	76	20	56
Taiwan SE Corp.	566.1	30	30	0
Thailand SE	332.6	13	13	0
Tokyo SE Group	N/A	68	65	3
Europe—Africa—Middle East				
Amman SE	606.9	18	18	0
Athens Exchange	15.8	4	3	1
BME Spanish Exchanges	21,726.2	192	191	1
Börsa Italiana	5,930.8	33	33	0
Budapest SE	9.5	3	1	2
Cairo & Alexandria SEs	866.8	20	20	0
Cyprus SE	279.9	4	4	0
Deutsche Börse	N/A	65	62	3
Euronext	13,329.9	46	30	16
Irish SE	2,159.9	9	7	2
Istanbul SE	3,372.8	9	9	0
JSE	0.0	62	54	8
Ljubljana SE	1,233.0	4	4	0
London SE	50,026.2	411	270	141
Luxembourg SE	265.7	20	1	19
Malta SE	42.4	2	2	0
Mauritius SE	0.0	7	6	1

(Continued)

Exhibit 1.4   (*Continued*)

| | | | Newly Listed Companies 2007 | |
Exchange	(US$ millions) Initial Public Offering	Total	Domestic Companies	Foreign Companies
OMX Nordic Exchange	6,057.4	94	90	4
Oslo Bors	1,778.4	30	24	6
Swiss Exchange	1,265.7	N/A	N/A	N/A
Tehran SE	505.4	9	9	0
Tel Aviv SE	2,707.4	64	61	3
Warsaw SE	5,486.4	105	93	12
Wiener Börse	2,337.1	9	7	2

COMPETITION SOURCES

Competition to U.S. exchanges arises primarily from three sources:

1. The London Stock Exchange (AIM), Hong Kong Stock Exchanges, Shanghai Stock Exchange, and other major foreign exchanges.
2. The use of Rule 144A IPOs. These private sales of equity securities to large institutional investors by both foreign companies and U.S. companies are thereafter listed for trading on alternative nonpublic markets, such as the GS Tradable Unregistered Equity OTC Market (GS TRuE) sponsored by Goldman Sachs & Co.
3. The difficult regulatory, legal (including litigation), accounting, and activist shareholder environment in the United States, which adversely affects the IPOs of smaller companies in particular.

The increasing prominence of foreign stock exchanges was illustrated by the announcement in July 2008 that the common shares of NYSE Euronext Inc., which owns the NYSE, would also be listed on the Shanghai Stock Exchange at the same time its common shares are traded on a European and U.S. exchange.[19]

The remainder of this chapter focuses on the use of Rule 144A IPOs and the problems of small-cap IPOs in the United States.

RULE 144A IPOS

Prior to 2007, private sales under Rule 144A to large institutional investors (called "qualified institutional buyers") by both foreign and U.S. companies was not considered an alternative to a publicly traded IPO. However, the development of alternative trading systems by major investment banks has created an alternative private IPO market. For example, in May 2007, Oaktree Capital Management LLC, a leading private U.S. hedge fund advisory firm, sold a 15% equity stake in itself for $880 million.[20] The deal was unusual because it was not structured as an IPO but rather a private placement to generally institutional investors holding more than $100 million of securities under Rule 144A of the Securities Act of 1933 (1933 Act). The stock was then traded on GS TRuE. This structure enabled the company to market and sell securities through an IPO that was not subject to the registration provisions of either the 1933 Act or the Securities Exchange Act of 1934 (1934 Act) and therefore was not subject to the burdensome provisions of SOX and related SEC regulations.

In August 2007, Apollo Management LP, a well-known private equity fund advisor, sold a 12.5% stake for $828 million in a similarly structured Rule 144A transaction, and the stock was subsequently traded by the institutional investors on GS TRuE.[21] In July 2007, Apollo sold 10% each to Calpers and to the Abu Dhabi Investment Authority, for a total of $1.2 billion.

In 2007, the Rule 144A offerings by U.S. issuers raised an amount greater than the amount raised in U.S. public offerings.[22] One academic has characterized this as a "paradigm shift" in the securities markets and a trend toward deretailization.[23] In effect, investors in the retail market are being increasingly foreclosed from the ability to invest in new IPOs.

SMALL-CAP IPOS

The IPO market for larger companies in the United States, either through traditional IPOs on the NYSE or Nasdaq or through private sales under Rule 144A, contrasts sharply with the IPO market for smaller companies. Few, if any, smaller companies would be of interest to large institutional investors for a Rule 144A transaction in the United States. Traditional IPOs for smaller companies have become very difficult in the United States.

When the post-IPO market valuation of a company is below $250 million, the advantages of the U.S. stock markets begin to decrease and materially decrease when the post-IPO market valuation is below $100 million. Many large institutional investors will not consider investments in companies having a post-IPO market valuation of less than $250 million. It becomes much more difficult to obtain coverage of the stock by securities analysts. These problems are exacerbated when the post-IPO market capitalization is below $100 million. The risk of the smaller U.S. public company becoming a so-called orphan (i.e., not followed by any securities analysts) is very real.

A 2006 study stated:

> In the United States a small company has to pay too much in fees and discounts when it sells its stock to the public. A small company selling fifty million dollars of its equity . . . [in] an IPO with a market value [at the end of first day] of over fifty-three and a half million, can net [after five million dollars of underwriting discounts and other fees and expenses] only forty-five million dollars in cash or less, a seventeen percent or more charge. Moreover, perversely those who charge to do the IPOs, underwriters, are uninterested in the smaller offerings; underwriters do not make enough money on the small offerings to justify their expenditure of time on them. A small company that wants to raise twenty-five million dollars cannot find an underwriter; a fifty million dollar IPO is a practical minimum.[24]

A 2000 GAO report stated:

[A]ccording to investment bankers we interviewed, businesses doing IPOs of less than $50 million generally are having a difficult time attracting large investment banking firms (e.g., Merrill Lynch and Goldman Sachs) to underwrite their public offerings. The investment bankers said this is the case partly because of high, fixed costs, including high, after-market monitoring costs and the need to make large-size investments. Therefore, these IPOs are commonly distributed by third- and fourth-tier investment banks rather than prestigious first-tier investment banks. Investors are less inclined to invest in small offerings placed with lower-tier investment banks because such firms often do not have the same market recognition that the large firms command. Further, we were told that another problem for these small issues is finding a securities analyst to cover the stock. In addition, investment bankers said that economies of scale typically make IPOs under $50 million uneconomical for larger investment banking firms.[25]

Smaller U.S. private companies may wish to consider an IPO outside of the United States. Prior to electing an international IPO, however, smaller U.S. private companies should consider an IPO in the country, even if the IPO is effectuated with a lower-tier underwriter on the OTC Bulletin Board or on the so-called Pink Sheets or through a reverse merger into a public shell (Chapter 12) or with a so-called SPAC (special-purpose acquisition company), discussed in Chapter 13. However, if none of these alternatives is feasible, an international IPO offering should be considered.

PROBLEMS OF SMALL-COMPANY IPOS

Smaller U.S. private companies face these problems in planning for an IPO in the major U.S. securities markets (each of which will be explored in more depth in this chapter):

- Significant accounting cost of complying with complex U.S. generally accepted accounting principles (GAAP) and SEC materiality rules, compared to more flexible international accounting standards

- Requirements to have a significant number of expensive independent directors on the board of directors, typically at least three on the audit committee and a majority of the board if the post-IPO company is not considered a "controlled company," in contrast to much less stringent requirements on international exchanges
- Expansive and burdensome SEC post-IPO reporting requirements, compared to the less detailed reporting requirements for international IPOs, which results in greater legal, accounting, and internal compliance costs for U.S. IPOs

These expensive requirements generally do not exist with respect to international IPOs. Many of these U.S. requirements are the result of the corporate corruption scandals (e.g., Enron and WorldCom) in the early twenty-first century that led to waves of new corporate governance requirements. Although scandals involving major public companies outside the United States occasionally occur (e.g., Parmalat), the international standards have not been changed to the same degree as the U.S. IPO standards.

The changes in the U.S. rules come from many sources, including the Financial Accounting Standards Board, the Public Company Accounting Oversight Board, the U.S. Securities and Exchange Commission, the NYSE, Nasdaq, and the pressures from activist shareholders, including hedge funds.

SEC'S ROLE

The SEC has, in particular, adopted burdensome disclosure regulations affecting small U.S. IPOs by failing to adequately distinguish between large and small public companies. The U.S. Regulatory Flexibility Act[26] requires the SEC to analyze the effect of its proposed regulations on "small entities." The SEC dutifully does so, generally with only minor and typically meaningless concessions to the problems of small businesses. Unfortunately, this statute does not require the analysis of the *cumulative* effect of all SEC rules on small businesses, only the particular regulation being adopted.

The cumulative effect of all of the SEC rules is to inflict on U.S. small businesses the equivalent of death by a thousand cuts. The result has been that the legal and accounting costs of complying with SEC rules are so large for many small businesses that they either (a) are forced to seek private equity to become large businesses before attempting an IPO, or (b) must abandon any exit through an IPO and consider only a sale exit. In the SEC's defense, some of its more burdensome rules have been the result of SOX and other pressures from the U.S. Congress.

The SEC should follow the example of the Tel-Aviv Stock Exchange, which has special rules for R&D companies that need to raise capital in their early stages. An R&D company is a company that has invested at least NIS 3 million (approximately $833,000) in research and development over the last three years, including investments using funds received from the Office of the Chief Scientist at the Israel Ministry of Industry and Trade. These R&D companies are permitted to offer their shares to the public under very lenient terms.[27]

These complex and burdensome SEC regulations have increased the post-IPO legal and compliance costs for all public companies substantially. However, the increased regulatory burden is much more material to smaller public companies. There are other reasons for the increase in U.S. accounting costs in addition to SEC regulations, as discussed next.

ACCOUNTING COSTS IN THE UNITED STATES VERSUS INDIA

The author asked these questions of a partner of a Big 4 accounting firm in Mumbai (Bombay), India, on March 21, 2008:

Q1. For an identical accounting service in India versus the United States, how much of a discount should be expected?

A1. The costs of accounting services in India vary significantly between the Big 4 firms and local firms. My guess is that costs associated with accounting and audit services from a Big 4 firm in India would generally be at a 50–60% discount to comparable services from a Big 4 firm in the United States.

Q2. For an identical company to have an IPO in India versus an IPO in the United States, could you guess how much less the accounting cost would be in India by percentage?

A2. My guess is that the accounting cost would be lower by approximately 65–75%.

Q3. For an identical company that has an IPO in India versus the United States, could you guess how much less the accounting cost would be in India for yearly accounting services subsequent to the IPO? Please use percentages.

A3. My guess is that the cost would be lower by approximately 60–70%.

Obviously, the discount from U.S. accounting costs would vary with each country. If too many IPO companies seek Indian accountants, it is likely that Indian accounting costs will rise in the future.

WHY ARE U.S. ACCOUNTING COSTS SO HIGH?

According to the Final Report of the Advisory Committee on Smaller Public Companies created by the SEC, external audit fees for smaller public companies roughly tripled as a percentage of revenue between 2000 and 2004. Fees for smaller public companies as a percentage of revenue have remained many times higher than for larger public companies over this period.[28]

Numerous factors caused the rise of U.S. accounting costs for public companies. These include:

- The demise of Arthur Andersen LLP
- More rigorous auditing and materiality standards
- Greater complexity of U.S. GAAP compared to international financial reporting standards

- Section 404 of SOX
- Higher compensation for accounting professionals in the United States

The confluence of each of these trends has resulted in the perfect storm insofar as accounting costs are concerned.

DEMISE OF ARTHUR ANDERSEN LLP

The demise of Arthur Andersen LLP was a wake-up call to all accountants and auditors. If the life of a major international accounting firm could be terminated, then all accounting firms were at risk. Each accounting firm tightened its auditing standards and modified the risk profile of the companies with which it would become associated to exclude riskier companies.

Smaller private companies planning an IPO typically have a higher risk threshold than larger private companies planning an IPO. Accounting items that would be immaterial to a larger private company can be very material to a smaller private company. Accordingly, smaller private companies are more frequently rejected for U.S. IPOs by the largest and most prestigious accounting firms.

The demise of Arthur Andersen LLP resulted in the centralization of power within the major accounting firms. Prior to the Arthur Andersen implosion, local accounting partners of major auditing firms could make decisions on significant matters without checking with the national office. That has all changed. Currently, local partners cannot make any significant decisions concerning their audit clients without running it by their "national" office. Although the centralization of power within the national office is understandable, it has resulted in additional layers of accounting review and further increased accounting costs.

The centralization of power in the national office of major accounting firms has not been as significant in dealing with foreign public companies. Many of the foreign offices of major accounting firms are given greater power to make significant accounting decisions. This is partly due to the perception of a less risky environment outside the

United States for accountants. It is also the result of the greater flexibility contained in international accounting standards than in U.S. GAAP, as will be discussed.

MORE RIGOROUS AUDITING AND MATERIALITY STANDARDS

The U.S. corporate corruption scandals embarrassed the accounting profession and created public pressure for more rigorous audits of public companies.

The SEC exacerbated this problem by developing the concept of "qualitative" materiality as well as "quantitative" materiality. At one time accountants believed that items that had an accounting effect less than 5% could be viewed as immaterial. That view was exploded in 1999, when the SEC issued Staff Accounting Bulletin (SAB) No. 99. Under SAB 99, items that were less than the 5% rule of thumb could be viewed as qualitatively material. Take, for example, this passage from SAB 99:

> The staff is aware that certain registrants, over time, have developed quantitative thresholds as "rules of thumb" to assist in the preparation of their financial statements, and that auditors also have used these thresholds in their evaluation of whether items might be considered material to users of a registrant's financial statements. One rule of thumb in particular suggests that the misstatement or omission of an item that falls under a 5% threshold is not material in the absence of particularly egregious circumstances, such as self-dealing or misappropriation by senior management. The staff reminds registrants and the auditors of their financial statements that exclusive reliance on this or any percentage or numerical threshold has no basis in the accounting literature or the law. . . .
>
> . . . The shorthand in the accounting and auditing literature for this analysis is that financial management and the auditor must consider both "quantitative" and "qualitative" factors in assessing an item's

materiality. Court decisions, Commission rules and enforcement actions, and accounting and auditing literature have all considered "qualitative" factors in various contexts. . . .

. . . Among other factors, the demonstrated volatility of the price of a
registrant's securities in response to certain types of disclosures may
provide guidance as to whether investors regard quantitatively small
misstatements as material. Consideration of potential market reaction
to disclosure of a misstatement is by itself "too blunt an instrument to
be depended on" in considering whether a fact is material. When, however, management or the independent auditor expects (based, for example, on a pattern of market performance) that a known misstatement
may result in a significant positive or negative market reaction, that expected reaction should be taken into account when considering whether
a misstatement is material.

SAB 99's identification of possible "market reaction" as another
factor in determining materiality to a corporate development created
great difficulty in application for accountants and attorneys. The requirement to at least consider market reaction substantially increased
the cost of accounting determinations. Accountants must consult with
their national office on close issues and in all likelihood will require
an attorney's opinion, further increasing the cost to the small U.S. public company.

GREATER COMPLEXITY OF U.S. GAAP

Corporate corruption scandals have also resulted in greater pressure on
U.S. accounting standards to permit fewer choices by management.
According to a Report on a Survey of Audit Committee Members con-
ducted by the Center for Audit Quality, an affiliate of the American
Institute of CPAs, 78% of those audit committee members surveyed
thought that audited financial statements were "too complicated."[29]
The Financial Accounting Standards Board has been active in is-
suing rule-based accounting standards that rival the U.S. Internal

Revenue Code (Code) in complexity. These detailed standards are designed to limit management choices. However, some of these standards contain major ambiguities. These require further interpretations that create additional complexity. The March 2008 survey of public company audit committee members, conducted by the Center for Audit Quality (an affiliate of the American Institute of CPAs), produced this interesting comment by one audit committee member:

> The current model has intricate rules that are not necessarily based on economics but rather the whims of overly technocratic rule makers, and what compounds the problem is that the investment bankers are smarter and more nimble than the rule maker.[30]

The complexity of U.S. GAAP is compounded by the tendency of the SEC Accounting Staff to strictly interpret the ambiguous wording of GAAP accounting pronouncements and second-guess the determinations of Big Four auditing firms. For example, the SEC Accounting Staff's interpretation of the requirements for segment reporting are so strict that public companies have been forced to create, for accounting purposes, business segments that they never internally use, solely in order to satisfy the SEC accountants.

Experts at the Big Four accounting firms believe that the SEC will ultimately mandate the use of international financial reporting standards (IFRS) for U.S. publicly traded companies due predominantly to the desire to have uniform worldwide accounting standards and in part to the perception that U.S. accounting standards may have become too complex. The SEC's chief accountant stated that the United States will shortly be the only country in the world not using IFRS and that the SEC will have to move toward IFRS by 2011.[31] In August 2007, the SEC published a proposed IFRS roadmap.

IFRS tends to be a more principle-based, rather than rule-based, accounting system and is currently much easier to apply. However, it is likely that IFRS will become more complex, detailed, and rule-based as U.S. GAAP is melded with IFRS.[32]

SECTION 404 OF THE SARBANES-OXLEY ACT OF 2002

Section 404 of SOX requires an auditor attestation report on the internal controls of public companies. The Public Company Accounting Oversight Board (PCAOB) published Auditing Standard No. 2, which, according to at least one SEC commissioner, was "much too granular"[33] and created a whopping increase in already inflated accounting costs. To its credit, the PCAOB has now substituted a less "granular" standard by adopting Auditing Standard No. 5. However, that standard is not inexpensive to apply, particularly for a smaller public company.

The SEC has postponed the auditor attestation report provision of Section 404 for smaller public companies for a number of years. However, it seems clear that at some point it will be applied and will significantly increase the costs of being a public company in the U.S.

IPO standards adopted outside the United States have generally rejected the auditor attestation requirement of Section 404. In speaking to officials in India and China, it seems clear that they have no intention of inflicting the Section 404 fiasco on their public companies. Likewise, the London Stock Exchange, including the AIM, has not adopted Section 404 requirements. In fact, the marketing literature for the AIM touts the absence of Section 404 as a major advantage of that market.

The corporate corruption scandals that motivated SOX were the result of fraud by chief executive officers (CEOs) and chief financial officers (CFOs). It is unclear how Section 404 mitigates this risk, since internal controls can be overridden by the CEO or the CFO. The SEC has conceded as much in SEC Release No. 33-8810 (June 27, 2007), which contains this revealing comment:

> ICFR [internal control over financial reporting] cannot provide absolute assurance due to its inherent limitations; it is a process that involves human diligence and compliance and is subject to lapses in judgment and breakdowns resulting from human failures. *ICFR also can be circumvented by collusion or improper management override.* Because of such limitations, ICFR cannot prevent or detect all misstatements,

whether unintentional errors or fraud. However, these inherent limitations are known features of the financial reporting process, therefore, it is possible to design into the process safeguards to reduce, though not eliminate, this risk. (Emphasis added.)

Despite this concession, the SEC has, to date, rejected the recommendation of its own Advisory Committee on Smaller Public Companies that certain small public companies be exempted from the requirement for an auditor attestation report on internal controls under Section 404 until a "framework for assessing internal control over financial reporting for such companies is developed that recognizes their characteristics and needs."[34]

Is it possible that public company requirements outside the United States will ultimately include an auditor attestation report on internal controls? Anything is possible, especially if there is repetition of international corporate corruption scandals, such as Parmalat. However, even if the standards are tightened in the future, it is doubtful that regulators outside the United States will repeat the same mistake as the U.S. regulators.

HOW TO IMPROVE THE COMPETITIVENESS OF THE U.S. CAPITAL MARKETS

It is important for both U.S. politicians and regulators to recognize that the world is increasingly "flat" insofar as the capital markets are concerned. While no one disputes the necessity of reasonable regulation of the capital markets, such regulation must take into account the potential off-shoring of the capital raising process.

Outside of the United States, small companies can raise substantially less than $5 to $10 million of capital from the public and still have their stocks traded on the country's stock exchange. For example, in October 2007, Allied Computers International (Asia) Limited engaged in the business of assembling and marketing laptop computers, had an IPO on the Bombay Stock Exchange (BSE), and raised approximately $1.5 million, with a market capitalization after the IPO of less than $6 million.

To be competitive in an increasingly flat world, the United States must develop a similar system. The SEC should encourage the major U.S. exchanges to develop a junior venture exchange similar to the AIM or the Canadian TSX Venture Exchange (see Chapter 9).

The SEC formed an Advisory Committee on Smaller Public Companies and then failed to adopt most of its recommendations, although it did adopt a few. To make the United States more competitive, the SEC should adopt all of the very modest recommendations contained in the Final Report of this committee.

AUDITOR'S ATTESTATION REPORT ON INTERNAL CONTROLS

Despite the almost universal rejection of requiring an independent auditor's attestation report on internal controls, which is provided for in Section 404 of SOX, the SEC continues to insist on imposing this requirement on smaller public companies. To its credit, the SEC has postponed the effective date of the auditor's attestation report several times.

The SEC has also conceded, as noted, that having good internal controls would not necessarily have prevented top management override of internal controls, such as occurred at WorldCom.

The SEC should continue to delay the requirement of an independent auditor's attestation report on internal controls for smaller public companies until it can determine with certainty that the cost of such a report would be financially immaterial to smaller public companies.

SEC REPORTING REQUIREMENTS

The twenty-first-century corporate corruption scandals proved that adopting more detailed and complex SEC disclosure rules will not prevent fraud. Fraudsters will always ignore SEC disclosure rules. Neither Enron nor WorldCom paid any attention to the SEC disclosure rules. However, the burdensome SEC disclosure rules, some of which were adopted in response to these scandals and SOX, do serve to deter IPOs by small businesses.

The SEC disclosure requirements for small businesses should, in general, not be any more burdensome to the small public company than the AIM disclosure requirements. The SEC would do well to review the AIM disclosure rules for smaller public companies.

There is no reason for the SEC to impose quarterly reporting on small public companies through the Form 10-Q report since most securities analysts never follow small public companies and their stock typically is not listed on major stock exchanges. Indeed, one of the primary justifications for originally requiring Form 10-Q reports was the fact that major stock exchanges mandated the dissemination of quarterly information as part of their listing requirements.[35] Unfortunately, the Form 10-Q report requirement was imposed on small public companies even though they would not otherwise be required by listing rules to supply quarterly information. A semiannual report, such as required by AIM, should be sufficient. If the market insists on quarterly reporting, small public companies will respond to market pressures. Indeed, the SEC required only semiannual reports (Form 9-K) prior to the 1970s.

Similarly, the SEC has expanded the Form 8-K requirement to apply to a significant number of events, including entry into any "material" agreements (subject to minor exceptions). Since many agreements that are immaterial to a large company can be material to a smaller company, this requirement and other Form 8-K requirements are more burdensome to smaller public companies.

The SEC should review the annual reporting requirements for AIM-listed companies and attempt to conform its annual report on Form 10-K for smaller public companies more closely to these requirements.

Finally, smaller public companies should be given the option to use international financial reporting standards as an alternative to U.S. GAAP. AIM-listed companies already have this right.

STATE SECURITIES LAWS

Even when the SEC tries to be creative in facilitating capital raising by small private companies, state securities regulators refuse to go along. For example, in Regulation A offerings (discussed in Chapter 14), which permit a private company to raise up to $5 million during any 12-month period, the SEC adopted a provision permitting the private company to "test the waters" prior to incurring the cost of creating an official offering statement.[36] Unfortunately, securities regulators in many states refuse to adopt a similar exemption, as a result of which the test-of the-waters procedure cannot be used in many states. If SEC wishes to help smaller private companies to raise capital, it should request Congress to preempt state securities laws that interfere with this process.

The SEC needs to remove the barriers to smaller private companies going public through an Internet direct public offering which sold only to accredited investor registered with the SEC under the 1933 Act. This will require the SEC to request Congress to preempt obsolete state securities laws, including those states (e.g., Kansas) that have so-called merit reviews.[37] Many states that are not known as merit review states (such as Pennsylvania) nevertheless use ambiguous words in their statutes to impose merit review, particularly on small business offerings.

The U.S. Congress has already passed legislation that preempts the registration provisions of state securities laws. However, this legislation (Section 18 of the 1933 Act) was limited to companies large enough to be listed on the major U.S. stock exchanges. This left smaller companies that attempted to raise public growth capital at the tender mercy of 50 different state securities laws.

These state securities laws typically are administered by bureaucrats and politically active commissioners who are sensitive to public criticism if securities offerings they review cause investor losses. Consequently, they tend to take a paternalistic view toward securities offerings and have low risk tolerances. Since securities offerings by small businesses are typically risky investments, these state securities laws impose difficult, if not impossible, burdens on small businesses attempting to raise public growth capital, even if these small businesses are willing to fully disclose their risks to investors. Neither Intel nor Microsoft would likely have satisfied the merit review standards during their start-up phases.

Small business has been the engine for employment growth in the United States. We have stifled its ability to raise public growth capital on a national basis because of these state securities laws. Most such laws were adopted in the late nineteenth century and the early twentieth century. While attempts have been made to create uniform state laws (e.g., the Uniform Securities Act), and a number of states have registration by notification or coordination, in the twenty-first century, there is no reason to impose on small businesses that wish to raise public capital nationally the burdensome and expensive requirement to comply with the registration provisions of these laws or to be subjected to merit review. State securities commissions should be confined to enforcing the antifraud provisions of their statutes and should allow public offerings registered with the SEC to proceed without merit review or other interference.

This concludes the discussion of the pros and cons of a U.S. IPO. International IPOs (including AIM IPOs) are covered in Chapters 9 and 10.

Chapters 2 through 8 discuss advance planning techniques for an IPO candidate, regardless of whether the private company is located in the United States or internationally. We begin in Chapter 2 with the requirement to develop impressive management and professional teams. This chapter considers certain U.S. tax issues in structuring equity incentives that may not be applicable to international companies. International companies should consult their own tax advisors for the tax consequences of equity incentives.

NOTES

1. Jay Ritter and Ivo Welch, "A Review of IPO Activity, Pricing, and Allocations," *Journal of Finance* 57 (2002): 1795–1828.

2. S. Torstila, "The Clustering of IPO Gross Spreads: International Evidence," *Journal of Financial and Quantitative Analysis* (September 2003) citing a 2002 study by Ljungqvist et al., both of which can be found at http://www.ssrn.com/.

3. A. Ljungqvist, *Handbooks in Finance: Empirical Corporate Finance,* Chapter III.4: "IPO Underwriting," Salmon Center, Stern School of Business, New York University and CEPR, September 1, 2004.

4. A. Butler (University of Texas at Dallas) and H. Wan (University of South Florida), "Investment Bank Compensation and IPO Pricing," July 19, 2005.

5. See "Handbooks in Finance: Empirical Corporate Finance" at Note 3.

6. L. Tian (Peking University) and W. Megginson (University of Oklahoma), "Extreme Underpricing: Determinants of Chinese IPO Initial Returns," March 15, 2007, www.ssrn.com/.

7. See S. Arco, J. Black, and G. Owen "From Local to Global—The Rise of AIM as a Stock Market for Growing Companies," London School of Economic and Political Science, www.londonstockexchange.com/NR/rdonlyres/4B0DF62A-BE1E-44F5-8616-EA2891873F1D/0/AIMshortreport.pdf (accessed September 2007).

8. "World Stock Exchanges," *Globe Law and Business* (May 2007): 296.

9. See Responses to Survey in Appendix B.

10. Response from partner of Big Five accounting firm located in Mumbai, India.

11. Ibid.

12. See report entitled "The Competitive Position of the U.S. Public Equity Market," Committee on Capital Markets Regulation, December 4, 2007. See also, Ernst & Young, "Growth During Economic Uncertainty: Global IPO Trends Report 2008," www.ey.com.

13. See "A Review of IPO Activity, Pricing, and Allocations," at Note 1.

14. See "The Competitive Position of the U.S. Public Equity Market" at Note 12.

15. S. Schubert, Foreword, "World Stock Exchanges," *Globe Law and Business* (May 2007).

16. See "The Competitive Position of the U.S. Public Equity Market" at Note 12.

17. Ibid.

18. See World Federation of Exchanges Annual Report and Statistics (2007), www.world-exchanges.org/WFE/home.Asp?nav=ie.

19. Stephen Joyce, "NYSE Euronext Will Be First Traded Firm to List in U.S. and China, Niederauer Says," BNA, Inc. Securities Regulation & Law Report (July 28, 2008).

20. See "Moving the Market: Oaktree Stock Sale Completed," *Wall Street Journal,* May 23, 2007.

21. See "Apollo Raises $828 Million," *Wall Street Journal,* August 7, 2008.

22. Steven M. Davidoff, "Paradigm Shift: Federal Securities Regulation in the New Millennium 3," available at papers.ssrn.com/sol3/papers.efm?abstract_ id=1080087.

23. Ibid.

24. A. Oesterle, "The High Cost of IPOs Depresses Venture Capital in the United States," Ohio State University Moritz College of Law (August 2006).

25. U.S. General Accounting Office, Report to the Chairman, Committee on Small Business, U.S. Senate, *Small Business: Efforts to Facilitate Equity Capital* (2000).

26. See Title 5 of the United Code, sections 601–612.

27. See www.tase.co.il/TASEEng/Listings/IPO/ResearchandDevelopment Companies/.

28. See "Final Report of the Advisory Committee on Smaller Public Companies" (April 23, 2006), http://www.sec.gov/info/smallbus/acspe.shtml.

29. Report on the Survey of Audit Committee Member (March 2008), www.thecaq.org/.

30. Ibid.

31. *Seventh Annual Financial Reporting Conference*, at Baruch College in New York, May 1, 2008.

32. See S. Johnson, "Goodbye GAAP," *CFO* (April 1, 2008).

33. P. Atkins, "Remarks Before the SIA Industry Leadership Luncheon," June 8, 2005. http://www.sec.gov/news/speech/spch060805psa.htm

34. See "Final Report of the Advisory Committee on Smaller Public Companies" (April 23, 2006), at Note 28; See also, Campbell, "Pernicious Economic Rule in Limiting Small Business's Access to Capital," Social Science Research Network (June 6, 2008), www.ssrn.com.

35. Rel. 34-8683, Federal Register, Vol. 34, No. 173 (September 10, 1969).

36. Rule 254 under the 1933 Act.

37. W. Sjostrom, Jr., "Going Public through an Internet Direct Public Offering: A Sensible Alternative for Small Companies?" *Florida Law Review,* Vol. 53, 529 et seq. (2001).

Part One

Advance IPO Planning

Chapter 2

Develop an Impressive Management and Professional Team[1]

Underwriters look for companies with impressive management teams. Reputable underwriters shy away from one-man or one-woman companies. They also avoid companies headed by inventors or technology experts who lack executive skills. It has been suggested that this was the reason Jim Barksdale became chief executive officer (CEO) of Netscape rather than Marc Andreesen.

The company's chief financial officer (CFO) must be an impressive as well as competent person and should preferably have public company experience. This is particularly true if the CFO will be the main contact person for investment analysts after the company's initial public offering (IPO). The IPO process requires an intense time commitment from the CFO as well as the CEO. During the IPO process the business must continue to run smoothly. Therefore, the company must develop personnel who will provide back-up for the normal functions that the CFO and CEO will not be available to perform during the IPO process.

The assembly of the management team should not occur on the eve of the company's IPO. If the company has a weakness in management, the time to upgrade its key employees is several years before its IPO target date. It may be prudent to obtain an objective evaluation of the company's management team by a reputable management consultant.

The company's auditor and attorneys must also be impressive to the investment community. The company should hire accounting firms and law firms that have the Securities and Exchange Commission (SEC) background and expertise to guide the company up to and through the IPO.

DEVELOPING INTERNAL ACCOUNTING EXPERTISE

The IPO process generally requires upgrading the company's internal accounting staff to include persons who have public company accounting experience. This should be accomplished well before the IPO target date so that the company's internal accounting systems can satisfy the more extensive disclosure and internal control requirements for a public company.

If the company is planning a U.S. IPO, the upgrading process, which can include both greater education of existing accounting staff as well as hiring accountants with public company backgrounds, can take a substantial amount of time. The U.S. IPO requires greater accounting expertise because of the complexities of generally accepted accounting principles (GAAP) and SEC accounting requirements.

COMPENSATION PACKAGES FOR THE MANAGEMENT TEAM

The company must develop compensation packages that will attract, retain, and motivate key employees who will form an impressive management team. The compensation package should have incentives that are tied to not only the annual budget but also a strategic plan.

Therefore, the company should develop a strategic plan well before the IPO. One of the goals of the strategic plan should be to grow the company sufficiently to become an attractive IPO candidate.

The compensation packages should include equity incentives for key employees. Equity incentives are extremely important to attract and retain key employees. These equity incentives can be tailored so that they do not vest unless and until there is an IPO or other event. The rest of the chapter is devoted to creating such equity incentives. The tax consequences of various equity incentives will depend upon the particular tax laws of each country. For purposes of simplicity, the remainder of this chapter discusses only federal income tax consequences under the U.S. Internal Revenue Code, as in effect on June 30, 2008.

OVERVIEW OF EQUITY INCENTIVES FOR KEY EMPLOYEES[2]

If a U.S. company wishes to grant equity incentives only to key employees, the company has five major choices:

1. Stock options, either incentive or nonqualified (with or without stock appreciation rights)
2. Stock appreciation rights, payable in stock or cash (or alternatively for limited liability companies, a "profits interest")
3. Performance share plans payable in stock or cash
4. Restricted stock bonus and award plans
5. Phantom stock plans payable in stock or cash

The term *phantom stock plans* is used in this book to refer to a wide variety of notional bonus plans including so-called performance share/ unit plans that are keyed to the increases in the value of the stock or other performance goals.

Some large companies permit their key employees to make their own selection among the various equity choices, so long as such choices have the same accounting charge attached to them. This is not necessarily the best practice since executives will tend to select time-restricted stock awards, which provide them with free stock if they are employed by the company through the vesting date even if the stock price during that period has not risen.

There is no universal single best choice for an equity incentive for executives of all companies. The exact equity incentive chosen depends on the culture and compensation philosophy of the company and its strategic plan. As previously noted, the terms of whatever equity incentive is chosen should be tied to the strategic plan. For example, if a company expects an exit within five years, the vesting of the equity incentive should coincide with the expected exit date or at least be accelerated by the exit event.

If an IPO is the intended exit event, key employees will likely have to execute lockup agreements with the underwriters. Therefore, an equity incentive plan should prevent equity vesting during the lockup period to avoid having taxable income being recognized for U.S. income tax purposes and to prevent problems under Section 409A of the U.S. Internal Revenue Code (Code).

Exhibit 2.1 provides a comparison of equity incentive plans that can be limited to key employees of a U.S. company.

A stock option permits an executive to acquire equity at or above the fair market value on the date of grant. As a result of Section 409A of the Code, options issued at exercise prices below the fair market value on the date of grant will be subject to a potential additional tax of 20%, bringing the maximum total federal income tax rate up to 55% (plus interest retroactive to the vesting date) from 35%. Therefore, it is no longer practical to issue stock options with exercise prices lower than the fair market value on the date of grant.

A stock appreciation right (SAR) typically permits the executive to receive the appreciation in equity over the grant date fair market value. For example, assume that the fair market value on the date of grant of the SAR is $10.00, the number of shares subject to the SAR is 100,000 shares, and upon exercise of the SAR three years later, the fair market value of the stock is $20.00 per share. The SAR therefore has a value of $1 million (100,000 shares multiplied by $10.00 appreciation per share) upon its exercise, and the executive would receive 50,000

Exhibit 2.1 Stock Option versus Stock Appreciation Rights

Incentive Stock Options	Nonqualified Stock Option Plans	Stock Appreciation Rights	Performance Share/Unit Plans	Restricted Stock Plans	Phantom Stock Plans
Description					
Right granted by employer to employee to purchase stock at stipulated price during specified period of time in accord with Section 422 of Internal Revenue Code.	Right granted by employer to employee to purchase stock at stipulated price over specific period of time.	Right granted to employee to realize appreciation in value of specified number of shares of stock. No employee investment required. Time of exercise of rights is at employee's discretion.	Awards of contingent shares or units granted at beginning of specified period. Awards earned out during period in which certain specified company performance goals are attained. Price of company stock at end of performance period (or other valuation criteria) determines payout value.	Shares of stock subject to restrictions on transferability with substantial risk of forfeiture. Shares granted to employee without cost (or at bargain price).	Employees awarded units (not any ownership interest) corresponding in number and value to specified number of shares of stock.

(Continued)

Exhibit 2.1 (Continued)

Incentive Stock Options	Nonqualified Stock Option Plans	Stock Appreciation Rights	Performance Share/ Unit Plans	Restricted Stock Plans	Phantom Stock Plans
Characteristics					
Option price is not less than fair market value on date of grant.	May be granted at price below fair market value.*	May be granted alone or in conjunction with stock options.	Awards earned are directly related to achievement during performance period.	Shares become available to employee as restrictions lapse—generally upon completion of a period of continuous employment.	Award may be equal to value of shares of phantom stock or just the appreciation portion.
Option must be granted within 10 years of adoption or shareholder approval, whichever is earlier, and granted options must be exercised within 10 years of grant.	Option period is typically 10 years. Vesting restrictions are typical. Previously acquired company stock may be used as full or partial payment for the exercise of nonqualified stock options.	Specified maximum value may be placed on amount of appreciation that may be received. Distribution may be made in cash or stock or both in amount equal to the growth in value of the underlying stock.	Performance periods are typically from three to five years. Grants usually are made every one to two years as continuing incentive device. Payments are made in cash or stock or combination.	Individual has contingent ownership until restrictions lapse. Dividends can be paid or credited to employee's account.	Dividend equivalents may be credited to account or paid currently. Benefit can be paid in cash or stock or both.
$100,000 limitation on total amount that first becomes exercisable in a given year (measured on date of grant)	May be granted to nonemployees.	May be granted to nonemployees.	May be granted to nonemployees.	May be granted to nonemployees.	May be granted to nonemployees.

Previously acquired stock may be used as payment medium for the exercise of incentive stock options.

Written approval of shareholders (within 12 months before or after adoption).

Employer

No tax deduction allowed to employer on exercise.	Tax deduction in the amount, and at the time, the employee realizes ordinary income.	Tax deduction in the amount, and at the time, the employee realizes ordinary income.	Tax deduction in the amount, and at the time, the employee realizes ordinary income.	Tax deduction in the amount, and at the time, the employee realizes ordinary income.	Tax deduction in the amount, and at the time, the employee realizes ordinary income.

Accounting Considerations

Fair value accounting under FAS 123R.	Fair value accounting under FAS 123R.	Fair value accounting under FAS 123R.	Fair value accounting under FAS 123R.	Fair value accounting under FAS 123R.	Fair value accounting under FAS 123R.

*Options granted at price below fair market value create Section 409A issues. See Chapter 13.

shares upon exercise of the SAR. In contrast to a stock option, the executive receives the 50,000 shares pursuant to the exercise of the SAR without having to pay an option exercise price of $10.00 per share.

If under these same facts a stock option had been granted with an exercise price of $10.00 per share on the date of grant, the executive would be out of pocket for $1 million in order to exercise the option and would have received 100,000 shares pursuant to the option exercise. One may argue that it is better to have the executive pay the $1 million option exercise price, thereby forcing him or her to use some personal funds to invest in the company. However, that is not the way stock options work. What typically happens is that the option exercise is "cashless," with the broker selling enough shares to fund the option exercise price (i.e., selling 50,000 shares at $20.00 per share), leaving the executive with a balance of 50,000 shares. This is exactly the same number of shares that the executive would have received under the SAR.

The effect of using the stock option is that the company has more shares outstanding in the marketplace, in this case 100,000 shares (50,000 shares sold by the broker and 50,000 shares held by the executive), whereas only 50,000 additional shares are outstanding under an SAR. (This example ignores any tax issues resulting from the exercise of the SAR or the stock option.) In view of the smaller dilution to existing shareholders arising from an SAR, using SARs instead of stock options may be viewed as a best practice.

Why then, you may ask, were so many stock options issued in the past rather than SARs? The answer is that the accounting rules have changed. Prior to FAS 123R, the current accounting rule, there was no charge to income from the grant of an option that satisfied the requirements of APB 25 (namely an exercise price equal to at least fair market value on the date of grant and time vested), whereas there was a charge to income for an SAR and so-called variable accounting could produce a large charge against income depending on the stock price. All of that has changed with the adoption of FAS 123R, which produces the same accounting result for a stock option or an SAR.

The disadvantage of an SAR to the executive is the absence of any potential federal long-term capital gains treatment for the appreciation in the stock, as more fully discussed later with respect to incentive stock options. Many executives who are granted incentive stock options never achieve long-term capital gains treatment for one of three reasons:

1. To avoid alternative minimum tax, the executive sells or otherwise makes a disqualifying disposition of the stock received under an incentive stock option in the year of exercise.
2. The executive sells or otherwise makes a disqualifying disposition of the stock before the end of the required holding period for an incentive stock option because of the need for cash.
3. The size of the option grant exceeds the $100,000-per-year limitation contained in Section 422(d) of the Code for incentive stock options.

Although SARs may also be settled in cash as well as equity, for purposes of this book, the preference is for those SARs that are settled solely in stock. A phantom stock plan that rewards the executive solely for appreciation in stock value above the grant date stock value, and that is settled solely in stock, is the equivalent of an SAR. For purposes of this book, we call this a *phantom appreciation plan.*

BEST PRACTICE: If the choice is between stock options and SARs that are settled solely in stock, SARs are preferable because they involve less dilution to shareholders.

RESTRICTED STOCK VERSUS SARS OR PHANTOM APPRECIATION PLANS

Restricted stock plans provide for the actual grant of shares of stock to executives and other employees, without cost to the grantee, subject to restrictions on transferability and to a substantial risk of forfeiture.

The substantial risk of forfeiture can consist of the continuation of employment for specified time periods, the satisfaction of certain performance goals, or both. Executives who make an election on Section 83(b) of the Code and pay the appropriate amount of federal income tax can achieve long-term capital gains on the appreciation at the time the forfeiture provisions lapse.

One advantage of restricted stock is that, if the company stock loses value, the executives really share the loss. This is in contrast to an SAR or stock option. If the SAR goes underwater (i.e., the SAR base price is above the current trading price) or if the exercise price of the stock option exceeds the current trading price, the executives do not suffer the same loss as they would if they held restricted stock.

The disadvantages of a restricted stock plan compared to an SAR or phantom appreciation plan are listed next.

- The executive becomes a shareholder immediately and is entitled to the rights and privileges of a shareholder, which includes the rights to dividends, as opposed to an SAR, which is merely an option and does not entitle the executive to any rights as a shareholder.
- The restricted stock rewards executives who have not contributed to the past growth of the company; in contrast, an SAR rewards employees only for appreciation in the value of the company after the SAR grant date.
- The grant of restricted stock increases the issued and outstanding stock and reduces basic earnings per share, whereas the SAR is reflected only in fully diluted earnings per share.
- Restricted stock that is vested solely by time (i.e., the executive must work for a certain number of years for the forfeiture provisions to lapse) rewards executives even if the value of the company does not increase or in fact goes down; in contrast, an SAR or stock option rewards the executive only for increases in value.

To avoid some of the disadvantages of restricted stock, some companies have inserted performance goals that must be satisfied in order for the restrictions to lapse. The Exxon Mobil Corporation, while not requiring performance goals, has a very long vesting period. For most of their senior executives, 50% of each grant of restricted stock is subject to a 5-year restricted period, and the balance is restricted for 10 years or retirement, *whichever is later.* In addition, the company provides a ceiling on annual restricted stock awards so that the overall number of shares granted represents a dilution of only 0.2%.

Some companies use restricted stock as a substitute for cash compensation, particularly start-up companies that have cash flow problems. More developed companies that may not be paying a competitive salary also may use restricted stock as a cash substitute. Private equity firms typically use restricted stock as a management retention incentive.

PHANTOM PLANS

A phantom plan is a notional plan that typically consists of a document that creates an equity equivalent award to the executive. A bookkeeping account typically is maintained for each award. The equity equivalent award usually is subject to vesting conditions and, when vested, may be settled in stock, cash, or some combination. The vesting conditions may involve just the continuation of the executive's employment for a specific time period. An example would be a phantom award of 1,000 units that vest at the rate of 20% per annum and are convertible into an equal number of shares of common stock upon vesting. This phantom plan would be similar to a grant of restricted stock that is time vested but would not have the disadvantage of a restricted stock award, which typically provides the executive with all the rights of a shareholder.

The greatest advantage of a phantom plan is the ability to defer federal income taxation until cash or shares are actually delivered or are constructively received by the holder of the phantom units (except that payroll taxes may be due upon vesting). The award of phantom units settled in shares uses fewer shares than an SAR or stock option to deliver equivalent value. The principal disadvantage to the executive of phantom units is that he or she would not have voting or dividend rights; however, the award may include a dividend equivalent feature.

Time-vested phantom plans reward the executive merely for continuing employment with the company, without regard to the accomplishments of either the executive or the company. The typical time-vested phantom plan does not require the payment of any exercise price. This contrasts with stock options that require the executive to pay an amount equal to the fair market value at the date of grant.

A time-vested phantom plan (similar to a time-vested restricted stock award) rewards the executive even if there has been no appreciation in the equity since the grant of the phantom award. The reward is given solely for continuing employment with the company.

Phantom plans can also contain performance conditions, as can stock options and SARs. For example, the phantom plan may require as a condition to vesting not only that the executive remain with the company, but that the company or the executive achieve certain financial goals. Phantom plans can also be made similar to an SAR or stock option by rewarding the executive only for appreciation in the stock value after the grant date.

Many phantom plans also contain so-called dividend equivalent rights. This is also a bookkeeping entry that credits the executive with additional phantom units based on cash dividends paid by the company prior to vesting. This is a desirable clause for companies with a high dividend payout that reduces the potential appreciation of the equity.

> **BEST PRACTICE:** Dividend equivalent rights for the holder of phantom stock should be considered when the company maintains a high dividend payout that impairs the appreciation of the equity.

ISOS VERSUS NON-ISOS

The advantage of an incentive stock option (ISO) is that it permits key employees to achieve long-term capital gain treatment on the

appreciation of the stock after the grant date, provided two requirements are satisfied:

1. The stock is not sold or otherwise disposed of in a "disqualifying
   disposition" for two years after the option grant and for one year
   after the exercise date.
2. The option holder is an employee of the company at all times from
   the grant date until three months prior to the exercise of the stock
   option (one year in the case of death or "disability" as defined in
   the Code).

Scenario 9.1. Executive Joe received an ISO grant on January 1,
2008, for 5,000 shares of common stock, at an exercise price of $5 per
share (its fair market value at the grant date). The option becomes fully vested in 5 years and expires in 10 years. Joe continues to be employed by the company until January 2, 2013, and he exercises his
fully vested option on February 1, 2013 (while still employed), at the
price of $5 per share. Joe sells the stock on February 2, 2014 at the
price of $25 per share. Joe would treat the $20 per-share gain as long-
term capital gain for federal income tax purposes and be taxed at a
15% rate (assuming long-term capital gains rate remains the same as
year 2008). If Joe had sold the stock on February 2, 2013, at $25 per
share, the $20 per share gain would be treated as ordinary income,
because Joe sold the stock within 1 year after exercise.

If Joe qualifies for long-term capital gains by selling on February 2,
2014, the company does not obtain a federal income tax deduction for
this $20 gain per share. If Joe receives ordinary income treatment be-
cause he sold on February 2, 2013, the company would obtain a federal income tax deduction for the $20 per share due to the ordinary
income recognized by Joe.

If the company is a C corporation in the 35% federal income tax
bracket, the company loses a deduction that would lower its federal
income taxes by $7.00 per share. If the company is a Subchapter S
corporation (S corporation) and the shareholders are in the 35% federal income tax bracket, the shareholders lose a tax deduction worth

$7.00 per share to the company (35% × $20). Tax flow through limited liability companies produces similar tax results.

The cost of giving Joe long-term capital gains in this example is the *loss* to the company (or shareholders of an S corporation and equity holders of a limited liability company) of federal income tax savings of $7.00 per share. The answer remains substantially the same if we factor in state income taxes.

How much does Joe benefit by having long-term capital gains on the appreciation? Answer: A lot less than the company (or shareholders of an S corporation or equity holders of a limited liability company) loses. If Joe would have paid federal income tax of 35% had the gain been ordinary income, and instead pays a 15% long-term capital gain on the $20 appreciation, Joe saves only 20% of $20, or $4.00 per share.

Is it worthwhile for the company (or shareholders of an S corporation) to give up a federal income tax deduction of $7.00 per share so that Joe can save $4.00 per share? The answer is probably no. For this reason, many public companies grant non-ISOs instead of ISOs.

Still, that is not the end of the story.

ADVANTAGE OF ISOS

Most employees will not satisfy the 1-year holding period on ISOs—they cannot afford to hold the stock for 1 year after paying the exercise price. Many highly paid executives can afford to hold the stock for the 1-year holding period. Nonetheless, doing so may subject these executives to paying alternative minimum taxes that apply to ISOs. As a result, many executives make disqualifying dispositions of stock acquired under ISOs in the year of exercise in order to avoid alternative minimum tax.

Consequently, by granting an ISO, the company can give an employee the *potential* of long-term capital gains treatment, but in most cases that is not the reality. When an employee makes a sale or other disqualifying disposition of the stock within 1 year after option exercise, the company (and or the shareholders of an S corporation or equity holders of a limited liability company) will generally obtain the same income tax deduction as if the employee originally received a non-ISO.

Moreover, if an employee receives a non-ISO and exercises it, the company will have to withhold on the exercise date an amount sufficient to pay the employee's federal income tax withholding and the employee's share of other payroll taxes on the share appreciation (unless the shares are subject to vesting conditions, in which case the tax is postponed until the vesting conditions are satisfied or a Section 83(b) election is made). Using an ISO avoids the result, since there is no withholding tax on an employee's exercise of the ISO.

The author of this book generally recommends that ISOs be issued to employees rather than non-ISOs, because they give the employee at least the potential of long-term capital gains treatment. Even though the employee will in most cases not achieve that potential because of personal sale decisions, the ISO generally is viewed as a more valuable option by knowledgeable employees who will avoid all federal withholding on option exercise.

Section 422(d) of the Code limits the amount of long-term capital gains that an employee can receive on an incentive stock option. The limitation is measured each calendar year by multiplying the option price of the incentive stock options received by the optionee by the number of option shares that first become exercisable during that calendar year. To the extent that this multiplication exceeds $100,000 in any calendar year, the excess numbers of shares are not entitled to long-term capital gains treatment.

NON-ISOS WITH TAX REIMBURSEMENT

A few companies have opted to grant non-ISOs with tax reimbursement to executives and other employees. The tax reimbursement assists employees in paying the federal income tax withholding upon exercise of the non-ISO. Nevertheless, there is withholding due on the tax reimbursement itself, so that the tax reimbursement must be sufficient to permit employees to pay withholding on both the exercise of the non-ISO and the tax reimbursement.

Scenario 9.2. In the previous example, suppose executive Joe received a non-ISO, which he exercised on January 2, 2013, and there was appreciation of $20 per share. Assume further that the required federal income tax withholding is 28%, or $5.60. Under these circumstances, Joe should receive tax reimbursement of approximately $7.78 per share, which, after tax withholding of 28% of that amount, would result in Joe receiving $5.60 per share. The $7.78 tax reimbursement to Joe should ordinarily be deductible by the company. The net after–federal income tax benefits to the company (or shareholders of an S corporation or equity holders of a limited liability company, assuming they are in the 35% federal income tax bracket) on the non-ISO exercise, after subtracting tax reimbursement, would be $1.94 per share. (See Exhibit 2.2.)

Exhibit 2.2 Computation of Federal Income Tax Benefit

$7.00	Federal income tax benefit of non-ISO tax deduction (35% × $20 per share)
+2.72	Federal income tax benefit of tax reimbursement (35% × $7.78 per share)
$9.72	
−7.78	Less cash cost of tax reimbursement
$1.94	Net cash federal income tax benefit

Thus, the company (or the shareholders of an S corporation or equity holders of a limited liability company) save $1.94 per share using a non-ISO in this example, *even after reimbursing Joe's federal income tax withholding.* If we factor in state income taxes, the answer remains substantially the same.

There is a slight difference in the tax result between ISO stock sold prematurely and a non-ISO. If on the exercise date of an ISO the appreciation is $20 per share and Joe sells the stock the next day at a price that produced a gain of $19 per share (the market value dropped $1), the company's federal income tax deduction (or the shareholders' deduction in an S corporation) and Joe's ordinary income tax is limited to the $19 gain per share. However, if Joe receives a non-ISO, Joe is taxed on the $20 per share gain on the date of exercise and the sale at $1 less produces a short-term capital loss for Joe for federal income tax purposes. In this case, the company's federal income tax deduction (or the shareholders' deduction in an S corporation or equity holders of a limited liability company) equals the $20 recognized by Joe on the date of exercise of the non-ISO.

A federal income tax reimbursement provision works only if the company pays federal income taxes. If the company has losses or loss carryovers, there are no current federal income tax savings from the exercise of a non-ISO. The tax deduction from the exercise of the non-ISO would only increase the company's loss carryovers.

If Joe executive is given an ISO and violates the 1-year holding period, the company's federal income tax savings (or the savings of the shareholders of an S corporation or equity holders of a limited liability company) is even greater than $1.94 per share and equals $7.00 per share (35% × $20). This is the same tax benefit as if Joe executive received a non-ISO without any tax reimbursement whatsoever.

The use of tax reimbursement provisions with non-ISOs requires the company to accrue the liability under the tax reimbursement provision on its statement of income for accounting purposes.

TAX BENEFIT TO THE COMPANY

The company receives a federal income tax deduction equal to the amount of income realized by its employee when he or she exercises a non-ISO or when they sell or make another disqualifying disposition of stock previously acquired within one year after exercising an ISO. These savings can be quite substantial. If the company is a Subchapter S corporation or an equity holder of a limited liability company, these tax deductions accrue to the personal benefit of the shareholders or equity holders, respectively.

Section 162(m) of the Code limits, in the case of a publicly held corporation, the tax deductions available to the company with respect to certain employee remuneration to the extent that the remuneration for a taxable year exceeds $1 million. This provision is applicable to the CEO (or an individual acting in such a capacity) and the four highest compensated officers (other than the CEO).

These federal income tax deductions have in the past eliminated all of the federal income tax of both Microsoft and Cisco Systems.[3]

SECTION 409A

The complex provisions of Section 409A of the U.S. Code and the final regulations under that section require companies to structure their equity incentives (and any amendments) so that they can rely on one of several exemptions from Section 409A.[4] In general, incentive stock options and employee stock purchase plans under Section 423 of the Code are exempted from Section 409A.

Chapter 3 deals with the methods of growing the company's business to qualify it for an IPO.

NOTES

1. Portions of this chapter are taken from *Executive Compensation Best Practices* (Hoboken, NJ: John Wiley & Sons, Inc. 2008).

2. See note 1.

3. G. Morgenson, "The Consequences of Corporate America's Growing Addiction to Stock Options," *New York Times,* June 13, 2000.

4. See Jane Jeffries Jones and Bryan Tyson, "Effect of Final Code Section 409A Regulations on Equity Plans," June 14, 2007, Womble Carlyle Sandridge & Rice, www.wcsr.com.

Grow the Company's Business with an Eye to the Public Marketplace

Growing the business with an eye to the public marketplace requires the company to become familiar with publicly held companies similar to its own business. If the company is engaged in two or more businesses, it should become familiar with other publicly held companies in each of the industries in which its businesses operate.

The company should pay particular attention to the price/earnings multiple of similar public companies. The company can find the trailing price/earnings multiple by dividing the market price of the stock by the earnings per share for the prior four quarters. This figure is regularly published in most financial newspapers.

If the price/earnings multiple of one of the company's two businesses is very low and that of the other business is much higher, the company should focus its attention on growing the business with the higher price/earnings multiple. The company's growth efforts will receive greater reward by concentrating on the business with the most potential.

Underwriters are particularly interested in businesses that are dominant in their fields. Again, focus the company's efforts on becoming dominant in a niche business.

INTERVIEWING POTENTIAL UNDERWRITERS

An excellent way to obtain some perspective on the company's potential for an initial public offering (IPO) is to interview potential underwriters several years before the company's IPO target date. Underwriters are usually interested in developing new relationships with pre-IPO candidates in hopes of generating consulting business or handling an IPO in the future. They usually will take the time to meet with management, even of early-stage companies with growth potential, to help educate them as to what types of companies would be attractive to the IPO market. The company should take advantage of these typically free educational sessions to help develop its own strategic growth plan leading to an IPO.

HOW LARGE MUST THE COMPANY BE TO QUALIFY FOR AN IPO?

Do you think that the company whose summarized financial information is presented in Exhibit 3.1 is a good or bad candidate for a traditional, firm-commitment IPO?

Exhibit 3.1   Selected Financial Information—1999

| | Fiscal Year Ending | | |
	1997	1998	First Quarter 1999
Product Revenues	$0	$43,000	$404,000
Net Loss	($622,000)	($9,117,000)	($4,264,000)

If you guessed that this company could not possibly qualify for a traditional IPO, you are wrong. This company, Drkoop.com, completed an $84 million public offering in June 1999. The lead underwriter was Bear, Stearns & Co., Inc., and the co-managers were Hambrecht & Quist and Wit Capital Corporation (as e-manager). Drkoop.com operated an Internet-based consumer healthcare network and is currently out of business.

Some would argue that the Internet offering mania of the late 1990s was an aberration in the IPO market. Therefore, let us consider the April 25, 2007, IPO of Orexigen Therapeutics, Inc., a biopharmaceutical company whose lead products targeted obesity. The lead underwriter was Merrill Lynch & Co., and their IPO raised $78 million net of underwriter discounts. Exhibit 3.2 shows financial information that is contained in the IPO prospectus.

Exhibit 3.2 Selected Financial Information—2007

	9/12/02–12/31/06	Year Ended December 31,				9/12/02–12/31/06
		2003	2004	2005	2006	
Total Revenue	$0	$0	$0	$262,367	$88,239	$350,606
Net Loss	($1,300)	($1,881,086)	($7,693,336)	($12,088,570)	($27,503,712)	($40,168,004)

Those who think that the IPO markets during the last years of the 1990s were unprecedented should consider the financial results of the company whose results are shown in Exhibit 3.3.

Exhibit 3.3 Selected Financial Information—1993

	Fiscal Year Ending			
	1989	1990	1991	1992
Net Sales	—	—	—	$53,890
Net Loss	$ (837,064)	$(1,489,026)	$(3,363,188)	$(3,492,703)

In February 1993, five years before the start of the Internet craze, the company just described in Exhibit 3.3 closed a $24 million IPO. The lead underwriters were Morgan Stanley Group, Inc., and Kidder, Peabody & Co., both prestigious underwriters. The company is named Cyberonics. Its business is to design, develop, and bring to market medical devices that provide a novel therapy, vagus nerve stimulation, for the treatment of epilepsy and other debilitating neurological disorders.

The larger underwriters generally require a minimum IPO of at least $50 million in order to permit them to earn a reasonable profit, and they prefer a post-IPO market capitalization (outstanding shares multiplied by share price) of at least $250 million to attract institutional investors. To achieve that level, the valuation of the company before receiving the IPO proceeds of $50 million must be at least $200 million.

Some underwriters *say* that they will not consider any company for an IPO unless it has income after taxes of at least $5 million during the last fiscal year. *The $5 million earnings level is really a rule of thumb that is often violated by those who advocate it.* In computing the $5 million earnings level, underwriters normally permit the company to add to its income the interest the company will save in paying off debt from the IPO proceeds.

Whether the company ever reaches the $5 million earnings level or not, it may still be a good IPO candidate. Many companies that have no earnings whatsoever, but great growth potential, go public with national underwriters. *The company's future growth potential is much more important to an underwriter than its current earnings.* Many national, regional, and local underwriters will underwrite a company's offering without regard to its earnings level.

Even very large and prestigious national underwriters occasionally underwrite a company with minimal or no earnings or large losses and great growth potential. This is particularly true in "hot" industries, but it is not limited to such industries.

Start-up companies with proven management teams are also taken public by prestigious underwriters. A "proven management team" means that it has successfully grown another company. For example, do you think that Bill Gates would have difficulty finding an underwriter if he started another company?

Exhibit 3.4 was compiled by members of the Securities and Exchange Commission (SEC) Office of Economic Analysis using public company data as of March 31, 2005.[1] More than 50% of the public companies had median market capitalization below $10 million; undoubtedly they included mostly OTC Bulletin Board and Pink Sheet companies.

Exhibit 3.4 Financial Information on SEC Reporting Companies—March 31, 2005

Revenue	No. Companies	Cumulative Percent of Companies	Median Market Capitalization (in millions)	Median Revenue (in millions)	Median Total Assets (in millions)
Up to $1m	724	10.7%	$10.6	$0.0	$1.7
$1m–$2m	147	12.9%	12.9	1.4	4.1
$2m–$5m	266	16.8%	12.9	3.3	5.6
$5m–$10m	287	21.1%	19.4	7.4	12.7
$10m–$20m	455	27.8%	34.0	14.6	22.4
$20m–$50m	837	40.2%	73.8	32.3	61.0
$50m–$100m	682	50.3%	149.3	69.2	104.9
$100m–$250m	846	62.8%	315.5	158.9	223.7
$250m–$500m	623	72.1%	602.5	351.8	460.3
$500m–$1b	591	80.8%	926.5	689.1	804.7
More than $1b	1,296	100.0%	3,508.2	2,826.2	3,665.1

GROWTH STRATEGIES

Reaching a high earnings level does give the company access to many more underwriters and reduces the percentage the company must sell in the IPO. Therefore, the company should develop a strategy to maximize its earnings.

The company's growth strategy might include expanding its product lines or entering into related businesses. This takes time. The company's strategy might also include a merger with another company in its industry. Some IPO candidates merge on the effective date of the

IPO. They fund the merger with the proceeds from the IPO or possibly use stock that is registered in the IPO.

Underwriters like companies that are showing growth through acquisitions. Identifying potential merger targets and negotiating transactions with them is not something easily done on the eve of the IPO.

Associating with a prestigious, professionally managed venture fund that will finance the company's growth can be an excellent IPO strategy. Institutional investors are more comfortable investing in a venture-backed IPO. These IPO investors tend to believe that the venture capitalists have thoroughly investigated the company before risking their own funds; therefore, they believe the company is a good IPO bet. One interesting study found that although the more reputable investment bankers were associated with significantly less IPO earnings management, there was no lessening of earnings management in venture-backed IPOs.[2]

Obviously, it is better to grow through bank loans and internally generated capital since the company avoids diluting its equity; however, that is not always possible. Identifying and negotiating with private capital investment sources takes careful advance planning. The company's growth strategy might require it to obtain additional private capital several years before the IPO target date.

SHOW EARNINGS OR REVENUE GROWTH BEFORE THE COMPANY GOES PUBLIC

Private companies typically are operated in a manner to minimize income taxes. As a result, they tend to adopt policies that reflect the lowest possible taxable income. If the company is in a hot market segment, such as Internet IPOs in the late 1990s, its current accounting earnings (if any) are probably irrelevant. Some of the Internet IPOs showed very little revenue, let alone earnings, and became successful IPOs as a result of the speculative fever generated by the growth prospects of the Web.

Investors are normally interested in the post-IPO growth of accounting earnings. If the company is not in a hot industry, its pre-IPO earnings growth is important to investors as a predictor of its post-IPO earnings growth. The company may have the greatest business in the world, but if it does not show its accounting earnings because of its minimization of taxes, the company will not get the best price for its stock when it does go public. The company may not even be able to have an IPO at all if it does not show sufficient earnings.

Underwriters also look at earnings trends to make certain that a consistent history of earnings growth over several years is reflected prior to the IPO. The investment community is justifiably suspicious of companies that show earnings for only one fiscal year just prior to the IPO target date.

Therefore, for at least two to three fiscal years prior to the company's IPO target date, it should begin showing earnings growth for financial accounting purposes. This is not always inconsistent with minimizing taxes, since different policies can be adopted for both tax and accounting purposes (e.g., taking accelerated depreciation for tax purposes but not for accounting purposes).

One method of reflecting accounting earnings is to reduce share-holder-officer salaries. If the shareholder-officers of the company do not want to reduce their lifestyle, the company should consider paying a dividend to make up for a shortfall. A dividend can have adverse tax effects if the company is not a Subchapter S corporation or a tax flow-through limited liability company. Therefore, the company, if it is a C corporation, should consider becoming a Subchapter S corporation as part of its IPO planning. (Other advantages to a Subchapter S election are mentioned in Chapter 8.)

ROLL-UPS AND OTHER ACQUISITIONS

A "roll-up" is a consolidation of a previously fragmented industry. The purpose of the consolidation is to create economies of scale. In many cases, professional management is installed.

Roll-ups come in three flavors:

1. Roll-ups before an IPO
2. Roll-ups after an IPO
3. Roll-ups simultaneously with an IPO

The third category, also known as "poof" roll-ups, involves the merger or other consolidation of a group of companies in the same industry that will be funded with the proceeds from an IPO. If the IPO occurs, the transactions are closed, and *poof!* we have a public company. The poof roll-up is a 1990s phenomenon. Examples of poof roll-ups are shown in Exhibit 3.5.

Exhibit 3.5   Poof Roll-ups

Company	Line of Business	Companies Acquired	Offering (millions)
UniCapital	Equipment leasing	12	$532.0
United Auto Group	Auto dealerships	7	187.5
Advanced Communications	Local exchange carrier	6	128.8
Group MAC	HVAC, plumbing	13	105.0
Integrated Electrical	Electrical contracting	15	91.0
Dispatch Management	Point-to-point delivery	41	79.5
Comfort Systems USA	HVAC services	12	79.3
Condor Technology	IT services	8	76.7
Medical Management	Physician management	5	66.0
USA Floral	Distribution of flowers	8	65.0
Metals USA	Processor of metals	9	59.0
Group 1 Automobile	Auto dealerships	30	57.6
Quanta	Electrical contracting	4	45.0
Compass International	Outsourced services	5	43.0
ImageMax	Document management	11	37.2

American business has a long history of entrepreneurs and financiers consolidating previously fragmented industries. For example, in the 1980s, large public companies emerged from previously fragmented industries as diverse as solid waste disposal, funeral services, and video rentals. Companies that emerged from this earlier phase of consolidation include: Paging Network Inc. (paging systems); WMX Technologies, Inc. (formerly Waste Management, Inc.) and USA Waste Services, Inc. (solid waste disposal); Service Corporation International (funeral services); and Blockbuster Entertainment Corporation (video rentals).

The roll-up phenomenon is not recent. Approximately 100 years ago, John D. Rockefeller did something similar when he founded Standard Oil.

STRATEGY OF ROLL-UPS

A roll-up is a method of increasing the valuation of the company's business by combining it with other businesses in the same industry. A roll-up is designed to increase the valuation of the company's business by:

- Permitting the company's business to grow large enough to qualify for an IPO, thereby achieving higher public company valuations
- Creating cost-saving efficiencies that further increase the company's combined income and further enhance the IPO valuation
- Increasing market penetration

Roll-ups permit greater market penetration, particularly in industries in which customers have multiple locations and prefer their suppliers to have the ability to service these multiple locations. Roll-ups of customers tend to beget roll-ups of their suppliers, since consolidated customers tend to have central purchasing and prefer dealing with single suppliers that can service multiple facilities.

Roll-ups can also be useful even in industries selling to retail customers or to business customers that do not have multiple locations. All other things being equal, these customers prefer dealing with larger, well-capitalized suppliers that will stand behind their product or service. Suppliers that are publicly traded companies with national operations have greater prestige, which may assist them in marketing customers.

PRIVATE COMPANY ROLL-UPS

A publicly traded company can effectuate a roll-up using either cash or its own marketable stock, or some combination.

However, it is difficult for a private company to effectuate a roll-up without cash. It is hard to induce someone to sell a business in exchange for stock of a privately held company, which provides no liquidity to the seller. Even if the privately held buyer agrees to repurchase its stock after five years if there is no IPO or sale, there is a risk that the privately held company may not be able to afford the repurchase after five years.

Because cash typically is required to effectuate private company roll-ups, it is not unusual for private companies to seek out private equity to supply these funds. Private equity, in turn, is attracted to the roll-up strategy since it may afford an excellent growth strategy if the roll-up is successful, with an exit of either an IPO or a sale.

Some privately held companies are able to effectuate their roll-up strategy using internally generated funds and normal bank financing. However, the minimum IPO size requirements make it difficult for most privately held companies to ramp up their size sufficiently to qualify for a higher-tier IPO underwriter without seeking outside capital.

Technically, a poof roll-up can be effectuated without a substantial amount of outside capital, since the mergers are completed with the cash proceeds from the IPO. However, a poof roll-up typically will require more than $2 million to cover the legal, accounting, and printing costs of these complicated transactions. Therefore, it is not unusual in these roll-ups to have the promoter fund these transaction costs and either to be reimbursed for these costs from the IPO or to receive a small equity percentage of the consolidated company to compensate them for the risk, or some combination of cash and stock.

The tendency of higher-tier underwriters of poof roll-ups to raise the minimum IPO size level for these transactions has further increased the transaction cost and encouraged the use of promoters with outside risk capital.

MEETING IPO SIZE REQUIREMENTS

Small to medium-size privately held businesses tend to have a valuation of four to seven times earnings before interest, taxes, depreciation, and amortization (EBITDA) less debt. The inability of these businesses to qualify for an IPO prevents them from achieving public company valuations, which can run 10 or more times EBITDA.

One primary reason that small-to-medium-size companies cannot qualify for an IPO is their size. To interest a higher-tier underwriter, the IPO must be sufficiently large to attract significant institutional interest. Most institutional investors want a minimum public company valuation, after the IPO is completed, of $250 million or more. Assuming that the underwriter is unwilling to sell more than 50% of the common stock in the IPO, this would require the private company to achieve a minimum valuation of at least $125 million before the IPO.

To achieve a post-IPO valuation of $250 million, most small and medium-size businesses must grow. A roll-up is one method of growing.

COST EFFICIENCIES

A well-structured roll-up permits cost savings for the combined enterprise. The cost-savings efficiencies result from:

- Reducing back office staff
- Increasing purchasing power
- Advertising efficiencies
- Eliminating duplicate locations
- Eliminating duplicate car and truck fleets
- Efficiencies in purchasing insurance, employee benefits, and administrative expenses
- Eliminating duplicate executives

The reduction in the administrative back-office staff is usually the primary cost saving efficiency in a roll-up. It is usually not necessary to grow the company's back-office staff in the exact same proportion as an increase in sales or revenues. As a result, the company's net income should rise after the IPO from these cost savings alone.

MULTIPLIER EFFECT

A well-structured roll-up into an IPO increases the company's valuation disproportionately to the actual revenue and income growth. Thus, if the company was worth 5 times EBITDA before the roll-up, it could be worth 10 times EBITDA in an IPO. This is true even though the combined income of the rolled-up companies has increased only slightly after the roll-up. The higher public company valuation versus the lower privately held company valuation plays the major role in this phenomenon.

In addition, the company's actual EBITDA should be disproportionately higher than the percentage increase in the company's pre–roll-up revenues as a result of the company's cost savings. These cost savings then are multiplied by the higher IPO valuation to increase the company's valuation.

The combined effect of the higher public company valuation plus the increased earnings due to cost savings can have a dramatic overall effect on the post–roll-up valuations, way out of proportion to what actually has been achieved in the roll-up. This disproportionate or multiplier effect is what drives the roll-up phenomenon.

SIMULTANEOUS OR POOF ROLL-UPS

Roll-up promoters who finance simultaneous or poof roll-ups obtain 10% to 15% of the total IPO shares as consideration. The earliest of these promoters were Jonathan J. Ledecky and Notre Capital Ventures II (Houston, Texas), but numerous other promoters have joined the business.

Mr. Ledecky created one of the earliest and largest roll-ups in U.S. Office Products Co. and has since created more, including USA Floral

Products, Inc., a flower distributor. Steven Harter, chairman of Notre Capital Ventures II, has completed a number of poof roll-ups, including: Coach USA, Inc., a roll-up in the motor coach industry; Comfort Systems, USA, Inc., which is consolidating the heating, ventilation, and air conditioning services industry; and Home USA, Inc., a consolidator of mobile home retailers.

These promoters typically interest a number of companies in the same industry in combining at the same time that an IPO occurs. If the IPO occurs, the merger closes, and *poof!* there is a public company.

These promoters typically offer each of the combining companies a combination of cash and stock in the public company. The rates vary with transactions and each promoter. A typical Notre transaction is 30% cash and 70% stock of the publicly held companies. The stock of the publicly held companies is not liquid and typically cannot be sold until at least one year and, in some cases, a longer time period or until the companies satisfy certain performance goals.

The percentage of stock and cash received by each of the rolled-up companies is usually negotiable, depending upon the promoter. It is not unheard of to have as much as 70% or more of the consideration payable in cash.

A chief executive officer from outside the combining companies typically will be hired to run the combined publicly held company.

COMMON MISTAKES IN ROLL-UPS AND OTHER ACQUISITIONS

A significant percentage of all acquisitions are unsuccessful. A study by a New York University professor has indicated that 65% fail. Roll-ups are not exempt from the risk of failure.

In some cases the failure is the result of bad timing, changes in the marketplace, bad luck, or other unforeseeable events. In other cases the failure was foreseeable.

As a general rule, the best acquisitions are made by one of two methods:

1. Buying a small division of a very large company

2. Buying a business in bankruptcy or on the verge of bankruptcy

A small division of a very large company typically is sold by personnel of the large company who have no motivation other than to prevent an accounting loss on the sale. As a result, a sale of assets at the book value of the assets, with no goodwill, is quite feasible. The book value of the assets may be substantially less than their real economic value.

Troubled company acquisitions are very difficult and complicated to complete but can prove to be the best values. The key is to have an experienced bankruptcy attorney who can protect the company from unwanted liabilities and claims. There is general agreement that the most common reason that roll-ups fail is because of the lack of an experienced management team to operate the combined companies, particularly in poof roll-ups after the IPO has been completed. However, many mistakes occur in the roll-up process prior to the IPO.

A few of the most common mistakes made in roll-ups and other acquisitions that are within the control of the acquiring entity are listed next.

Common Mistake No. 1. Failing to perform sufficient due diligence on the roll-up or acquisition target and devise a plan to manage different business cultures.

This is the most common cause of foreseeable failure. If the company does not regularly make acquisitions, it will need to assemble a sophisticated due diligence team to be certain that it is not overpaying for the target. There is no such thing as overdoing the company's due diligence.

The most common mistake in performing due diligence is the failure to understand the needs of the target's customers and their existing relations with the target's employees. At a minimum, representatives of the buyer should call on and personally visit the top five customers.

Existing personal relationships with the target's key employees must be explored thoroughly with the customers. If such relationships exist, these key employees must be given positive incentives to remain with the buyer and negative incentives to keep them from leaving the buyer (e.g., a covenant not to compete).

To the extent possible, the seller's motivations for selling should be understood. Many sellers decide to exit when they foresee problems ahead for the business.

It is very difficult to integrate different businesses together successfully. One of the major reasons for this problem is the various business cultures of each of the rolled-up companies.

Due diligence should uncover the cultural difference and help to develop a plan to better manage the different business cultures after the roll-up.

Common Mistake No. 2. Rolling up or acquiring a company whose financial statements will not satisfy the SEC, resulting in the postponement of the company's IPO.

In order to go public, the company normally will need audited financial statements for three full fiscal years prior to IPO filing. If the company's acquisition target does not have audited financial statements for the three-year period, the company will have to hold up its IPO until it can obtain such audits. It is not always possible to obtain such audits retroactively, particularly if the acquisition target maintains inadequate records or primarily sells from inventory.

Therefore, the company's auditors must be brought into the acquisition process at an early stage to make certain that the target's financial statements can satisfy SEC requirements. If the target acquisition's financial statements cannot pass muster, the company may be required to postpone the IPO for a many as three years, unless the target acquisition falls below certain materiality thresholds established by the SEC.

> **Common Mistake No. 3.** Relying too heavily on the target's audited financial statements.

When the target provides audited financial statements to the buyer, there is a tendency to have these reviewed by the buyer's accountants and to rely on the review to detect any issues that would affect the valuation of the target's business. The more prestigious the auditing firm for the target, the greater is the tendency of the buyer to rely on it.

There are three problems with such reliance:

1. In many states the auditor has no liability whatsoever to the buyer if the target's financial statements are in error, unless the target's auditors have specifically authorized the buyer to so rely.

2. Generally accepted accounting principles are extremely elastic. It is not possible to ferret out all of the actual accounting principles and practices just by reviewing the target's audited financial statements. Instead, a thorough review by the company's own auditor is essential.

3. The auditor for the target's financial statements is generally entitled to rely on the target's management's representation letter to the auditor. Therefore, even if the company purchases the stock of the target, the target's outside auditor can defend the buyer's lawsuit by claiming that it was misled by the fraud of the target's management.

> **Common Mistake No. 4.** Obtaining an inadequate escrow or holdback (e.g., notes) of the purchase price.

Possession of an escrow or holdback of the purchase price places the buyer in the driver's seat. If the buyer has a postclosing claim, the buyer can just refuse to pay the escrow or holdback amount.

Many sophisticated acquirers refuse to pay the target or its shareholders more cash than the book value of the target's net assets. The balance of the purchase price consists of notes. If the buyer has postclosing claims against the target or its shareholders, these notes can be offset by the claim amount.

If the escrow or holdback is nonexistent or is inadequate, collecting on claims against the target or its shareholders can be extremely expensive, time consuming, and frustrating. In some cases, after the target or its shareholders pay their taxes on the company's purchase price and their own attorney's fees, there can be very little left for the buyer to collect even if it wins its lawsuit. An arbitration provision in the purchase contract sometimes can be helpful in this regard by reducing litigation discovery expenses and avoiding the cost and delay of endless appeals. To be fully effective, the arbitration provision should prevent or severely limit prearbitration discovery and make the arbitrator's award nonappealable to the extent possible.

Common Mistake No. 5. If the company is the lead company in a roll-up, it should avoid paying the same earnings multiplier that it expects to receive in an IPO for significantly smaller companies in its industry.

For example, if the company expects to receive a multiplier of 10 times its next 12-month earnings projection in an IPO, a much smaller company in the roll-up should be priced at a reasonable discount from this multiplier, for example, 8. Otherwise, the company's only leverage from the consolidation results from the cost savings and efficiencies it can achieve. In some situations, it is not possible to realize these savings and efficiencies, at least initially. As a result, the company's post-IPO earnings may be flat, resulting in the marketplace punishing its post-IPO trading price.

VENTURE-BACKED IPOS

Many companies that wish an IPO exit will need private equity financing to grow their business prior to the IPO. Poof roll-ups, which can be financed with IPO proceeds, are relatively difficult to effectuate. In addition, it is hard to negotiate acquisitions when the sole consideration is in the form of the equity of the private company buyer. Accordingly, it is likely that acquisition growth prior to an IPO may require private equity financing.

The equity required to finance growth can be obtained in various ways, including obtaining financing from friends and family, from private placements to angel investors, from SPACS (see Chapter 13), and from professionally managed private equity funds.

It is likely that many pre-IPO candidates will require financing from professionally managed private equity funds. There are severe limits on financing from friends and family and from angel investors. There are certain advantages and disadvantages of obtaining private equity from a professionally managed private equity fund.

A list of the advantages and disadvantages of obtaining financing from a professionally managed private equity fund follows.

Advantages

- Private equity funds have deep pockets.
- The association of the company with a prestigious private equity fund makes it easier to attract an IPO underwriter. Venture-backed IPOs tend to have a lower failure risk.[3]
- A private equity fund will require the company to establish good internal controls and corporate governance. This will ultimately assist the company in its IPO.
- A good private equity fund will provide potential acquisition targets to the company, assist the company in its growth strategy, and introduce the company to IPO underwriters.

Disadvantages

- There is significant dilution of the equity interest of the founders of the company.
- Operational restrictions will be imposed on the company by the private equity firm, including certain veto rights on major transactions.

- The private equity fund may have different goals from the founders of the company and insist that the company be sold rather than exit through an IPO or follow-on offering.

The Orexigen IPO previously mentioned was venture-backed by these private equity funds: Domain Associates, LLC; Sofinnova Venture Partner VI, LP; FMR LLC; Scale Venture Partners II; and funds affiliated with Kleiner Perkins Caufield & Byers. Venture-backed companies have had a significant number of IPOs, as illustrated in Exhibit 3.6.

Exhibit 3.6   Venture-Backed U.S. IPOs

Year/Quarter	No. IPOs[*]	Total Offer ($M)	Average IPO Offer ($M)
2001	41	3,489.9	85.1
2002	22	2,109.1	95.9
2003	29	2,022.7	69.8
2004-1	13	2,721.1	209.3
2004-2	29	2,077.8	71.7
2004-3	24	3,225.6	134.4
2004-4	27	2,990.4	110.8
2004	**93**	**11,014.9**	**118.4**
2005-1	10	720.7	72.1
2005-2	10	714.1	71.4
2005-3	19	1,458.1	76.7
2005-4	17	1,568.1	92.2
2005	**56**	**4,461.0**	**79.7**
2006-1	10	540.8	54.1
2006-2	19	2,011.0	105.8
2006-3	8	934.2	116.8
2006-4	20	1,631.1	81.6
2006	**57**	**5,117.1**	**89.8**

[*]Includes all companies with at least one U.S. venture capital investor that trade on U.S. exchanges, regardless of domicile.

Source: Thomson Financial & National Venture Capital Association.

Chapter 4 deals with the primary deal-killer in IPOs: the failure of the company to have audited or auditable financial statements.

NOTES

1. www.sec.gov/info/smallbus/acspc/appendi.pdf.

2. Gemma Lee (University of Alabama) and Ronald W. Masulis (Vanderbilt University), "Do Underwriters or Venture Capitalists Restrain Earnings Management by IPO Issuers?," Social Science Research Network (March 17, 2008), www.ssrn.com.

3. Elizabeth A. Demers (University of Rochester) and Phillip Joos (Tilburg University), "IPO Failure Risk" (April 2006), www.ssm.com.

Obtain Audited or Auditable Financial Statements Using IPO-Acceptable Accounting Principles

Any company thinking about an initial public offering (IPO) in the future must be aware of the necessity of obtaining audited or auditable financial statements that use IPO-acceptable accounting principles. This is true whether the IPO will be in the United States or international.

The most common reason why IPOs are delayed is because the financial statements are not audited and cannot be audited or, even if audited, do not use IPO-acceptable accounting principles. The author has experienced numerous situations where the IPO was delayed because of the inability of the company to provide audited financial statements. However, even if the financial statements are audited by one of the so-called Big Four accounting firms, that is no assurance that they contain IPO-acceptable accounting principles. Some IPOs have been delayed by the Securities and Exchange Commission (SEC) so long, because of the failure to apply acceptable accounting principles, that the IPO window closed and the company was unable to raise capital.

The SEC normally requires audited income statements for three years in order for a company to go public, if the company or a predecessor has been in business that long. It may not be possible, on the eve of the IPO, to retroactively obtain audited financial statements. This is particularly true if sales of inventory account for a significant portion of the company's revenues and no auditor has ever observed the company's inventory.

Therefore, it is preferable to obtain either currently audited financial statements or "auditable" financial statements (i.e., financial statements that are capable of being audited retroactively at the time of the company's IPO). Waiting until the eve of the company's IPO to obtain audited financial statements can delay the IPO and cause the company to lose an IPO window. Therefore, start the audit at least six months before the company's proposed IPO filing date.

INTERNAL CONTROLS AND SYSTEMS

The company must have in place sufficient internal controls and systems to permit audited financial statements. For example, if the company is in a retail business and does not have an inventory management system in place, it is unlikely to be able to obtain audited financial statements. Good internal controls are necessary for any IPO candidate, a topic discussed more fully in Chapter 7.

USING IPO-ACCEPTABLE ACCOUNTING PRINCIPLES

If the company's IPO is in the United States, it should expect a very thorough review of the accounting principles utilized in the preparation of its financial statements. If the IPO is outside of the United

States, the accounting review will vary with the country and the sophistication of the regulators.

Many companies believe that because they use a Big Four accounting firm, their financial statements will pass muster with the SEC. Nothing can be further from the truth. Many of the local partners of Big Four accounting firms are not up to date on the latest SEC thinking. Indeed, only a few national partners at the Big Four accounting firms can really be called experts on the latest issues of interest to SEC accountants. Any company that is thinking about an IPO in the United States should insist that a national SEC partner thoroughly review the accounting principles and practices it followed well before the proposed IPO filing date.

The SEC provides on its Web site a document entitled "Current Accounting and Disclosure Issues in the Division of Corporation Finance." This document should be read carefully before any U.S. IPO in order to identify a few of the accounting issues that the company may face.

The remainder of this chapter is devoted to the one accounting issue that causes more problems than any other in IPOs: revenue recognition.

REVENUE RECOGNITION

The area most likely to cause accounting problems for the company will be in its revenue recognition policies: that is, at what point in the sale process the company is entitled to recognize revenue for financial statement purposes.

Satisfying the SEC's revenue recognition policies may require a change in the company's terms of sale for products and services. The sales terms can be crucial to the company's ability to recognize revenue for accounting purposes.

These examples, taken from SEC Staff Accounting Bulletin No. 104, illustrate a few of the issues in revenue recognition.

The staff believes that revenue generally is realized or realizable and earned when all of the following criteria are met:

• Persuasive evidence of an arrangement exists,[1]

• Delivery has occurred or services have been rendered,[2]

• The seller's price to the buyer is fixed or determinable,[3] and

• Collectibility is reasonably assured.[4]

Persuasive evidence of an arrangement

Facts: Company A has product available to ship to customers prior to the end of its current fiscal quarter. Customer Beta places an order for the product, and Company A delivers the product prior to the end of its current fiscal quarter. Company A's normal and customary business practice for this class of customer is to enter into a written sales agreement that requires the signatures of the authorized representatives of the Company and its customer to be binding. Company A prepares a written sales agreement, and its authorized representative signs the agreement before the end of the quarter. However, Customer Beta does not sign the agreement because Customer Beta is awaiting the requisite approval by its legal department. Customer Beta's purchasing department has orally agreed to the sale and stated that it is highly likely that the contract will be approved the first week of Company A's next fiscal quarter.

Question: May Company A recognize the revenue in the current fiscal quarter for the sale of the product to Customer Beta when (1) the product is delivered by the end of its current fiscal quarter and (2) the final written sales agreement is executed by Customer Beta's authorized representative within a few days after the end of the current fiscal quarter?

Interpretive Response: No. Generally the staff believes that, in view of Company A's business practice of requiring a written sales agreement for this class of customer, persuasive evidence of an arrangement would require a final agreement that has been executed by the properly authorized personnel of the customer. In the staff's view, Customer Beta's execution of the sales agreement after the end of the quarter causes the transaction to be considered a transaction of the subsequent period.[5] Further, if an arrangement is subject to subsequent approval (e.g., by the management committee or board of directors) or execution of another agreement, revenue recognition would be inappropriate until that subsequent approval or agreement is complete.

Customary business practices and processes for documenting sales transactions vary among companies and industries. Business practices and processes may also vary within individual companies (e.g., based on the class of customer, nature of product or service, or other distinguishable factors). If a company does not have a standard or customary business practice of relying on written contracts to document a sales arrangement, it usually would be expected to have other forms of written or electronic evidence to document the transaction. For example, a company may not use written contracts but instead may rely on binding purchase orders from third parties or on-line authorizations that include the terms of the sale and that are binding on the customer. In that situation, that documentation could represent persuasive evidence of an arrangement.

The staff is aware that sometimes a customer and seller enter into "side" agreements to a master contract that effectively amend the master contract. Registrants should ensure that appropriate policies, procedures, and internal controls exist and are properly documented so as to provide reasonable assurances that sales transactions, including those affected by side agreements, are properly accounted for in accordance with GAAP [generally accepted accounting principles] and to ensure compliance with Section 13 of the Securities Exchange Act of 1934 (i.e., the Foreign Corrupt Practices Act). Side agreements could include cancellation, termination, or other provisions that affect revenue recognition. The existence of a subsequently executed side agreement may be an indicator that the original agreement was not final and revenue recognition was not appropriate. . . .

Delivery and performance

a. Bill and hold arrangements

Facts: Company A receives purchase orders for products it manufactures. At the end of its fiscal quarters, customers may not yet be ready to take delivery of the products for various reasons. These reasons may include, but are not limited to, a lack of available space for inventory, having more than sufficient inventory in their distribution channel, or delays in customers' production schedules.

Questions: May Company A recognize revenue for the sale of its products once it has completed manufacturing if it segregates the inventory of the products in its own warehouse from its own products? May Company A recognize revenue for the sale if it ships the products to a third-party warehouse but (1) Company A retains title to the product and (2) payment by the customer is dependent upon ultimate delivery to a customer-specified site?

Interpretative Response: Generally, no. The staff believes that delivery generally is not considered to have occurred unless the customer has taken title and assumed the risks and rewards of ownership of the products specified in the customer's purchase order or sales agreement. Typically this occurs when a product is delivered to the customer's delivery site (if the terms of the sale are "FOB [free on board] destination") or when a product is shipped to the customer (if the terms are "FOB shipping point").

The Commission has set forth criteria to be met in order to recognize revenue when delivery has not occurred.[6] These include:

1. The risks of ownership must have passed to the buyer;

2. The customer must have made a fixed commitment to purchase the goods, preferably in written documentation;

3. The buyer, not the seller, must request that the transaction be on a bill and hold basis.[7] The buyer must have a substantial business purpose for ordering the goods on a bill and hold basis;

4. There must be a fixed schedule for delivery of the goods. The date for delivery must be reasonable and must be consistent with the buyer's business purpose (e.g., storage periods are customary in the industry);

5. The seller must not have retained any specific performance obligations such that the earning process is not complete;

6. The ordered goods must have been segregated from the seller's inventory and not be subject to being used to fill other orders; and

7. The equipment [product] must be complete and ready for shipment.

The above listed conditions are the important conceptual criteria that should be used in evaluating any purported bill and hold sale. This listing is not intended as a checklist. In some circumstances, a transaction may meet all factors listed above but not meet the requirements for revenue recognition. The Commission also has noted that in applying the above criteria to a purported bill and hold sale, the individuals responsible for the preparation and filing of financial statements also should consider the following factors:[8]

1. The date by which the seller expects payment, and whether the seller has modified its normal billing and credit terms for this buyer;[9]
2. The seller's past experiences with and pattern of bill and hold transactions;
3. Whether the buyer has the expected risk of loss in the event of a decline in the market value of goods;
4. Whether the seller's custodial risks are insurable and insured;
5. Whether extended procedures are necessary in order to assure that there are no exceptions to the buyer's commitment to accept and pay for the goods sold (i.e., that the business reasons for the bill and hold have not introduced a contingency to the buyer's commitment).

Delivery generally is not considered to have occurred unless the product has been delivered to the customer's place of business or another site specified by the customer. If the customer specifies an intermediate site but a substantial portion of the sales price is not payable until delivery is made to a final site, then revenue should not be recognized until final delivery has occurred. . . .[10]

Fixed or determinable sales price

a. Refundable fees for services

A company's contracts may include customer cancellation or termination clauses. Cancellation or termination provisions may be indicative of a demonstration period or an otherwise incomplete transaction. Examples of transactions that financial management and auditors should be aware of and where such provisions may exist include "side" agreements and significant transactions with unusual terms and conditions. These contractual provisions raise questions as to whether the sales price is fixed or determinable. The sales price in arrangements that are cancelable by the customer is neither fixed nor determinable until the cancellation privileges lapse.[11] If the cancellation privileges expire ratably over a stated contractual term, the sales price is considered to become determinable ratably over the stated term.[12] Short-term rights of return, such as thirty-day money-back guarantees, and other customary rights to return products are not considered to be cancellation privileges, but should be accounted for in accordance with Statement 48.[13]

Facts: Company M is a discount retailer. It generates revenue from annual membership fees it charges customers to shop at its stores and from the sale of products at a discount price to those customers. The membership arrangements with retail customers require the customer to pay the entire membership fee (e.g., $35) at the outset of the arrangement. However, the customer has the unilateral right to cancel the arrangement at any time during its term and receive a full refund of the initial fee. Based on historical data collected over time for a large number of homogeneous transactions, Company M estimates that approximately 40% of the customers will request a refund before the end of the membership contract term. Company M's data for the past five years indicates that significant variations between actual and estimated cancellations have not occurred, and Company M does not expect significant variations to occur in the foreseeable future.

Question: May Company M recognize in earnings the revenue for the membership fees and accrue the costs to provide membership services at the outset of the arrangement?

Interpretive Response: No. In the staff's view, it would be inappropriate for Company M to recognize the membership fees as earned revenue upon billing or receipt of the initial fee with a corresponding accrual for estimated costs to provide the membership services. This conclusion is based on Company M's remaining and unfulfilled contractual obligation to perform services (i.e., make available and offer products for sale at a discounted price) throughout the membership period. Therefore, the earnings process, irrespective of whether a cancellation clause exists, is not complete.

In addition, the ability of the member to receive a full refund of the membership fee up to the last day of the membership term raises an uncertainty as to whether the fee is fixed or determinable at any point before the end of the term. Generally, the staff believes that a sales price is not fixed or determinable when a customer has the unilateral right to terminate or cancel the contract and receive a cash refund. A sales price or fee that is variable until the occurrence of future events (other than product returns that are within the scope of Statement 48) generally is not fixed or determinable until the future event occurs. The revenue from such transactions should not be recognized in earnings until the sales price or fee becomes fixed or determinable. Moreover, revenue should not be recognized in earnings by assessing the probability that significant, but unfulfilled, terms of a contract will be fulfilled at some point in the future. Accordingly, the revenue from such transactions should not be recognized in earnings prior to the refund privileges expiring. The amounts received from customers or subscribers (i.e., the $35 fee mentioned above) should be credited to a monetary liability account such as "customers' refundable fees."

The staff believes that if a customer has the unilateral right to receive both (1) the seller's substantial performance under an arrangement (e.g., providing services or delivering product) and (2) a cash refund of prepaid fees, then the prepaid fees should be accounted for as a monetary liability. In consideration of whether the monetary liability can be derecognized, Statement 140 provides that liabilities may be derecognized only if (1) the debtor pays the creditor and is relieved of its obligation for the liability (paying the creditor includes delivery of cash, other financial assets, goods, or services or reacquisition by the debtor of its outstanding debt securities) or (2) the debtor is legally released from being the primary obligor under the liability.[14] If a customer has the unilateral right to receive both (1) the seller's substantial performance under the arrangement and (2) a cash refund of prepaid fees, then the refund obligation is not relieved upon performance of the service or delivery of the products. Rather, the seller's refund obligation is relieved only upon refunding the cash or expiration of the refund privilege.

Chapter 5 discusses other potential IPO deal killers that must be remedied well before the IPO target date.

NOTES

1. Concepts Statement 2, paragraph 63, states, "Representational faithfulness is correspondence or agreement between a measure or description and the phenomenon it purports to represent." The staff believes that evidence of an exchange arrangement must exist to determine if the accounting treatment represents faithfully the transaction. See also SOP 97-2, paragraph 8. The use of the term "arrangement" in this SAB topic is meant to identify the final understanding between the parties as to the specific nature and terms of the agreed-upon transaction.

2. Concepts Statement 5, paragraph 84(a), (b), and (d). Revenue should not be recognized until the seller has substantially accomplished what it must do pursuant to the terms of the arrangement, which usually occurs upon delivery or performance of the services.

3. Concepts Statement 5, paragraph 83(a); Statement 48, paragraph 6(a); SOP 97-2, paragraph 8. SOP 97-2 defines a "fixed fee" as a "fee required to be paid at a set amount that is not subject to refund or adjustment. A fixed fee includes amounts designated as minimum royalties." Paragraphs 26–33 of SOP 97-2 discuss how to apply the fixed or determinable fee criterion in software transactions. The staff believes that the guidance in paragraphs 26 and 30–33 is appropriate for other sales transactions where authoritative guidance does not otherwise exist. The staff notes that paragraphs 27 through 29 specifically consider software transactions; however, the staff believes that guidance should be considered in other sales transactions in which the risk of technological obsolescence is high.

4. ARB 43, Chapter 1 A, paragraph 1, and Opinion 10, paragraph 12. See also Concepts Statement 5, paragraph 84(g), and SOP 97-2, paragraph 8.

5. AU Section 560.05

6. See *In the Matter of Stewart Parness,* AAER 108 (August 5, 1986); *SEC v. Bollinger Industries, Inc., et al.,* LR 15093 (September 30, 1996); *In the Matter of Laser Photonics, Inc.,* AAER 971 (September 30, 1997); *In the Matter of Cypress Bioscience Inc.,* AAER 817 (September 19, 1996). Also see Concepts Statement 5, paragraph 84(a), and SOP 97-2, paragraph 22.

7. Such requests typically should be set forth in writing by the buyer.

8. See *In the Matter of Stewart Parness*, AAER 108 (August 5, 1986); *SEC v. Bollinger Industries, Inc., et al.*, LR 15093 (September 30, 1996); *In the Matter of Laser Photonics, Inc.*, AAER 971 (September 30, 1997); *In the Matter of Cypress Bioscience Inc.*, AAER 817 (September 19, 1996). Also see Concepts Statement 5, paragraph 84(a), and SOP 97-2, paragraph 22.

9. Such individuals should consider whether Opinion 21, pertaining to the need for discounting the related receivable, is applicable. Opinion 21, paragraph 3(a), indicates that the requirements of that opinion to record receivables at a discounted value are not intended to apply to "receivables and payables arising from transactions with customers or suppliers in the *course of business which are due in customary trade terms* not exceeding approximately one year" (emphasis added).

10. SOP 97-2, paragraph 22.

11. SOP 97-2, paragraph 31.

12. Ibid.

13. Ibid.

14. Statement 140, paragraph 16.

Cleaning Up the Company's Act

Public companies operate in a fishbowl. If the company engages in illegal or other questionable practices as a private company, it may have created contingent liabilities that may have to be publicly disclosed in the initial public offering (IPO) registration statement. It is difficult to sell the securities of a company that may have significant contingent liabilities resulting from questionable practices.

It is wise to stop any questionable practices many years before the company's IPO target date. Indeed, the statute of limitations on causes of action for commercial bribery or for understatement of federal income taxes (e.g., as a result of inventory cushions, paying relatives who do not work, etc.) may be as long as six years and could be even longer in certain cases.

It is strongly recommended that the company stop any such questionable practices well before the date it plans to go public. Besides, the company's directors and officers will sleep better at night.

IPO DEAL KILLERS

Typical examples of IPO deal killers if the resulting contingent liability is large in relation to the value of the company's business are listed next.

- Environmental liabilities
- Litigation liabilities
- Tax liabilities resulting from misclassification of employees as independent contractors
- Unfunded pension obligations and multiemployer pension plan liabilities
- Product warranty obligations of unreasonable scope of length
- Excessive insider transactions not at arm's length
- Violations of the U.S. Foreign Corrupt Practices Act of 1977 or similar international laws

The best example of an IPO that failed as a result of misclassification of employees as independent contractors was the 1998 IPO of the Mustang Ranch, a house of prostitution in Nevada. Although prostitution was perfectly legal in the counties of Nevada in which the ranch was located, the IPO failed when the U.S. Internal Revenue Service declared that the prostitutes were really employees of the Mustang Ranch rather than independent contractors and that the ranch owed a huge amount of payroll tax withholding. This was unfortunate since the IPO would likely have been oversubscribed as a result of trophy value of the stock certificates.

Google, Inc. was embarrassed because of illegal acts that had to be remedied in its IPO, which ultimately was successful. Google, Inc. issued stock to employees in excess of what the securities laws permitted without registration and was forced to make a rescission offer to its employees in its IPO prospectus.

It is recommended that the company's operations be reviewed for legal compliance well before the IPO target date. Under the U.S.

securities laws, underwriters have a due diligence obligation to carefully scrutinize the company before the IPO, or they could be liable for material misstatements or omissions in the IPO prospectus. The IPO underwriter will employ an attorney who will perform a detailed investigation of the company before permitting an IPO registration statement to be filed with the SEC with the underwriter's name on it.

U.S. FOREIGN CORRUPT PRACTICES ACT OF 1977 AND SIMILAR INTERNATIONAL LAWS

Recently, there has been increased enforcement of the U.S. Foreign Corrupt Practices Act of 1977 (FCPA), which has extraterritorial application in the global marketplace. A material violation of the FCPA can create major problems in an IPO. The civil and criminal penalties attached to violations of this law can create substantial liabilities. For example, in the spring of 2007, Baker Hughes Incorporated paid a total of $45 million for violating the FCPA, which consisted of a criminal fine, a civil penalty, a disgorgement of profits, and prejudgment interest resulting from a $5.2 million bribe of foreign officials in Kazakhstan.[1] Although the bribe was $5.2 million, the disgorgement of profits from the entire venture by Baker Hughes was $23 million, well in excess of the bribe.

In addition to the FCPA, the Organization for Economic Co-Operation and Development (OECD) Convention on Combating Bribery of Foreign Public Officials in International Business Transactions has resulted in the adoption of FCPA-type laws by a growing number of international jurisdictions. For example, India has its own version of the FCPA. Both the United Nations and the World Bank are also intensifying their anticorruption efforts, in addition to the efforts of the OECD and local law enforcement authorities.

The FCPA, which is enforced by both the SEC and the U.S. Department of Justice, amended the 1934 Act to impose certain accounting standards on public companies and to prohibit "corrupt" foreign payments by or on behalf of U.S. corporations (whether public or not), business entities, citizens, nationals, and residents. The FCPA was the result of SEC investigations in the mid-1970s, when over 400 U.S. companies admitted making questionable or illegal payments in excess of $300 million to foreign government officials, politicians, and political parties. The abuses ran the gamut from bribery of high foreign officials to secure some type of favorable action by a foreign government to so-called facilitating payments that allegedly were made to ensure that government functionaries discharged certain ministerial or clerical duties. The U.S. Congress enacted the FCPA to bring a halt to the bribery of foreign officials and to restore public confidence in the integrity of the American business system.

ACCOUNTING STANDARDS

Under the U.S. accounting standards, which are not applicable until after a U.S. IPO that causes the company's securities to be registered under the 1934 Act, the company is required to:

A. Make and keep books, records, and accounts that, in reasonable detail, accurately and fairly reflect the transactions and dispositions of the assets of the company; and

B. Devise and maintain a system of internal accounting controls sufficient to provide reasonable assurance that:

    i. Transactions are executed in accordance with management's general or specific authorization;

    ii. Transactions are recorded as necessary (a) to permit preparation of financial statements in conformity with generally accepted accounting principles or any other criteria applicable to such statements, and (b) to maintain accountability for assets;

    iii. Access to assets is permitted only in accordance with management's general or specific authorization; and

    iv. The recorded accountability for assets is compared with the existing assets at reasonable intervals and appropriate action is taken with respect to any differences.

The 1934 Act's requirements with regard to the maintenance of books and records and a system of internal control were enacted largely in response to disclosures that many U.S. corporations had established so-called off-the-book accounts and slush funds. However, they are applicable to all U.S. public companies, whether they engage in foreign business or employ slush funds or not.

It must be borne in mind that the accounting standards imposed by the 1934 Act are directed at the accuracy of the company's books, records, and accounts, not its financial statements. Thus, even though the company has not paid foreign bribes and even though its published financial statements may be accurate in all respects, it could nonetheless be in violation of the 1934 Act if, for example, its books and records improperly characterized the nature of a perfectly legitimate item of expense.

Section 404 of the Sarbanes-Oxley Act (SOX) and related SEC rules also govern internal controls and are applicable from the time an IPO registration statement is filed under the 1933 Act. The SEC's rule requires management to evaluate the effectiveness of the design and operation of the company's internal controls in each annual report that it is required to file under the 1934 Act. The SEC rule requires that the company's annual report contain an internal control report of management that includes:

- A statement of management's responsibilities for establishing and maintaining adequate internal control over financial reporting for the company.

- A statement identifying the framework used by management to conduct the required evaluation of the effectiveness of the company's internal control over financial reporting.

- Management's assessment of the effectiveness of the company's internal control over financial reporting as of the end of the company's most recent fiscal year, including a statement as to whether the company's internal control over financial reporting is effective. The assessment must include disclosure of any "material weakness" in the company's internal control over financial reporting identified by management. Management is not permitted to conclude that the company's internal control over financial reporting is effective if there are one or more material weaknesses in the company's internal control over financial reporting.

• A statement that the registered public accounting firm that audits the company's financial statements included in the company's annual report has issued an attestation report of the company's internal controls over financial reporting.

This SEC rule also requires an attestation report by the company's independent auditors, as noted in Chapter 1, except that this requirement currently does not apply to certain smaller public companies. In addition, management is required to report on any material changes to its internal controls on a quarterly basis.

FOREIGN BRIBES

The FCPA also proscribes and criminalizes foreign corrupt payments, as noted earlier. Generally speaking, the 1934 Act makes it illegal for any public company, as well as any officer, director, employee, or stockholder acting on behalf of the company, to pay, promise to pay, or authorize the payment of money or anything of value to:

• Any official of a foreign government or instrumentality of a foreign government;

• Any foreign political party;

• Any candidate for foreign political office; or

• Any person that the company knows or has reason to know will make a proscribed payment, or will promise to make or authorize payment of a proscribed payment

if the purpose is to induce the recipient to: (a) use his or her influence with the foreign government or instrumentality; (b) influence the enactment of legislation or regulation by that foreign government or instrumentality; or (c) refrain from performing any official responsibility, in each case, for the purpose of obtaining or retaining business for or with, or directing business to, any person.

In order to fall within the 1934 Act's proscriptions, the payment, or promise or authorization of payment, must be "corrupt"; that is, whether it is legal under the laws of the foreign jurisdiction or not, it must be intended to induce the recipient to use his official position for the benefit of the person offering the payment or his client. The 1934 Act prohibits not only the payment of, but also the promise or authorization of, a corrupt foreign payment. Therefore, the law can be violated even if the payment is never in fact made. Since a corrupt payment that is requested by the foreign official (rather than offered to him) involves a decision to accede to the request, it is not a defense that the payment was requested. However, payments that are extorted and are made to protect physical assets from capricious destruction are not within the ambit of the 1934 Act. In addition, so-called grease payments (e.g., payments to ministerial or clerical employees of foreign governments or agencies, to speed them in the performance of or encourage them to in fact perform their duties) are not prohibited by the 1934 Act.

It is clear that, if authorized, the making of a foreign corrupt payment by a foreign subsidiary of a U.S. company is prohibited by the 1934 Act. Even joint ventures with foreign companies are covered to some extent. Also prohibited are payments to an agent (even one who is not him- or herself subject to the 1934 Act) when it is known or should be known that they will be used to make corrupt payments.

If the company engages in foreign transactions, particularly those involving an agent, great care should be exercised to secure documentation to prove that the 1934 Act was not violated. It is prudent to secure an affidavit from any agents who are paid commissions attesting to their compliance with the 1934 Act. Obviously, such an affidavit is useless if company officials have reason to know that it is false.

Violations of the corrupt payment provisions of the 1934 Act are punishable by fines and civil penalties against corporations or business entities of up to $2 million ($10,000 civil penalty in an action brought by the SEC). In addition, officers, directors, employees, agents, and shareholders can be fined up to $100,000 (plus a $10,000 civil penalty in an action brought by the SEC) or imprisoned for not more than five years, or both, for violations of the corrupt payment provisions of the 1934 Act. The 1934 Act further provides that fines imposed on an individual violator cannot be paid, directly or indirectly, by the company for whose benefit the bribe was paid or promised.

RECENT EXAMPLES OF VIOLATIONS OF FOREIGN BRIBE PROVISIONS

The FCPA applies to bribes of "any official of a foreign government or instrumentality of a foreign government." In a number of countries, the government is an owner or partial owner of all sorts of ventures. In China, for example, the government is an owner or government officials are owners of what appears to be commercial ventures. That government ownership creates major issues from an FCPA perspective. For example, in May 2005, a wholly owned Chinese subsidiary of Diagnostic Products Corp. (DPC), a U.S.-based medical equipment firm, pled guilty to criminal charges arising out of approximately $1.6 million in sales "commissions" made by DPC, through its subsidiary, to doctors and laboratory staff employed by state-owned hospitals in China in order to generate business. The doctors and laboratory staff were considered officials of a foreign government or its instrumentality.[2]

The broad scope of the foreign bribe provisions of the FCPA is best illustrated by the next case dealing with travel and entertainment expenses for Chinese foreign officials.

In *SEC v. Lucent Technologies, Inc.*,[3] the SEC's complaint alleged that over a three-year period Lucent, through a subsidiary, paid over $10 million for about 1,000 Chinese foreign officials to travel to the

United States. The SEC concluded that about 315 of the trips had a disproportionate amount of sightseeing, entertainment, and leisure. Some of the trips were, in fact, vacations to places such as Hawaii, Las Vegas, the Grand Canyon, Disney World, and similar venues. These expenses for officials Lucent was either doing business with or attempting to do business with were booked to a factory inspection account. The company failed over the years to provide adequate FCPA training.

To resolve the SEC's case, Lucent consented to an injunction prohibiting future violations of the FCPA books and records provisions. In addition, the company agreed to pay a $1.5 million civil penalty.

The SEC action against the Dow Chemical Company in 2007[4] also involved the question of travel and entertainment expenses. In its complaint, the SEC alleged that a Dow subsidiary in India made improper payments to an Indian government official consisting of over $37,000 in gifts, travel, entertainment, and other items. Payments were also made to an official of the Central Insecticides Board to expedite the registration of three products. To resolve the SEC action, Dow consented to the entry of a permanent injunction prohibiting future violations of the books and records provisions of the FCPA. The company also agreed to pay a civil penalty of $325,000.

The next chapter answers installing anti-takeover defenses before the IPO.

NOTES

1. SEC Release Number 2007–77, April 26, 2007.
2. Securities Exchange Act of 1934 Release No. 51724, May 20, 2005.
3. *SEC v. Lucent Technologies, Inc.*, Civil Action No. 07-092301 (D.D.C. filed December 21, 2007).
4. *SEC v. The Dow Chemical Company*, Civil Action No. 07-00336 (D.D.C. filed February 13, 2007).

Chapter 6

Establish Antitakeover Defenses

The boards of directors of public corporations today are being faced with an array of challenges from hostile and activist shareholders. These shareholders range from hedge funds that would like to force the sale of the company to individual shareholders who have a social or corporate governance agenda. The company should, prior to its initial public offering (IPO), consider taking steps to protect itself and its board of directors from these pressures.

According to FactSet SharkWatch in 2007, 501 activist and other campaigns for corporate control were announced during the year, making it a 17% increase over 2006, in which there were 429 such campaigns.[1] The percentage of activist-related campaigns remained steady, with 35% of all campaigns announced in 2007 and 2006 having at least one SharkWatch50 member in the activist group. The SharkWatch50 member is a compilation of 50 significant activist investors. Inclusion in the SharkWatch50 is based on a number of factors, including the number of publicly disclosed activist campaigns at targeted companies.[2] Among the SharkWatch50, Steel Partners, LLC, was the most prolific, launching 14 activist campaigns since 1994. In 2007 it turned its attention to Japan.[3]

Even international companies are not immune from the hedge funds.[4] Eight of the Steel Partners, LLC, 14 campaigns announced were against Japanese companies. Ramius Capital Group, LLC, announced the most campaigns against U.S. companies with 10.

One article on hedge funds characterizes them in this way:

> Hedge funds are not "normal" institutional investors. They launch proxy fights for corporate control. Their recent successes and "wolf pack" tactics have garnered headlines.... An empirical survey found over 50 instances of hedge fund activism, and also found the terrorism effect of these examples to be considerable. The survey further found that the combination of "wolf pack" tactics and the increasing influence of activist proxy advisory firms (the recommendations of which many institutional investors follow automatically) have made hedge fund activists a real power in corporate governance.[5]

From a corporate governance viewpoint, the best protection against hostile shareholders is to develop a thoughtful long-term strategic plan and adhere to it. A long-term strategic plan developed by management and the board of directors permits the company to resist the efforts of investors with shorter horizons, such as hedge funds, from taking actions inconsistent with the strategic plan. Once developed, the strategic plan should be articulated to shareholders well before hedge funds or other hostile shareholders make any effort to pressure the company. A strategic plan first articulated after a company has been pressured by hostile shareholders tends to lack credibility and typically is viewed by investors as an antitakeover device. The compensation of executives should be tied to realizing the objectives of the long-term strategic plan as well as meeting year-to-year budgets.

Apart from the long-term strategic plan, there are many other steps a company can take prior to its IPO to protect itself from hostile and activist shareholders. It should be noted that so-called poison pill plans, which the board can adopt without shareholder approval, do not protect the company against hedge funds or other activist shareholders that wish to change the board of directors. Poison pill plans protect against a hostile takeover offer but do not affect the rights of shareholders to change the composition of the board of directors.

PLACE ANTITAKEOVER PROTECTIONS IN THE CHARTER

The charter of the company is the most important place to insert antitakeover protections prior to the IPO. The charter of a U.S. incorporated company typically is called the articles of incorporation or the certificate of incorporation. Many companies prior to their IPO place protection in their by-laws rather than in their charter. This is a mistake unless the charter limits a shareholder vote on by-law amendments.

The charter of a public company that is incorporated in the United States and many other countries generally can be amended only with a prior vote of the board of directors in addition to the shareholders. A charter cannot be amended by the vote of the shareholders alone without the prior vote of the board.

In contrast, in the United States and many other countries, by-laws can be amended by a vote of a majority of those shareholders who cast votes (either in person or by proxy) at a properly held shareholders' meeting, unless such amendment is otherwise restricted by the charter. Therefore, if 51% of all the shares are voted at a shareholders' meeting (either in person or by proxy), only 25.51% would be needed to pass the resolution of an activist shareholder, which resolution could include changes to the by-laws. In addition, if all of the shareholders did not cast votes who were present (in person or by proxy) at the shareholders' meeting, the required vote would be significantly less than 25.51%.

Hedge funds and other activist shareholders may attempt to change the by-laws of a public company by obtaining shareholder approval to install annual elections of directors (as opposed to staggered terms for directors) or to insert other by-laws provisions that pressure the board to make changes, spin-off divisions, or sell the company. Therefore, it is important to create the antitakeover protections in the charter or, alternatively, to at least insert a provision in the charter requiring a high vote (e.g., 75% of all shareholders) for shareholder-initiated by-law changes that have not been previously approved by the board.

STAGGERED TERMS FOR DIRECTORS

The laws of many states in the United States and in other countries permit directors to be classified and elected for staggered terms. The advantage of staggered terms for directors, as opposed to annual elections for all directors, is that it takes longer for a hedge fund or other activist shareholder to obtain control of the board of directors. For example, in Delaware, the board can be classified into three classes, with one-third of the directors elected each year. To change control, the board would require the hedge fund to win two annual elections. In Pennsylvania, the board can be classified into four classes, with one-fourth of the directors elected each year, which would require the hedge fund to win three elections to the board to obtain majority control.

Another significant advantage of having a classified board in the United States and certain other countries is that the shareholders cannot remove the board prior to the end of their terms except for cause. Cause typically is narrowly defined by the courts; therefore, this represents a significant antitakeover protection.

Again it is important to insert the protection of staggered terms in the charter and not in the by-laws, unless the charter contains protections against shareholder-initiated by-law changes.

Many U.S. underwriters will permit the charter of a company seeking an IPO to contain staggered terms for directors.

CREATING AUTHORIZED COMMON STOCK AND BLANK CHECK PREFERRED STOCK

Under most laws, the board of directors has the authority to issue shares of common stock that have been authorized for issuance in the charter without obtaining shareholder approval. Therefore, it is important to authorize a sufficient number of shares of common stock in the charter so that shares can be issued to "white knights" and other friendly parties in the event of a hostile takeover offer. Many exchanges, however, limit the number of shares that can be issued without shareholder approval as part of their listing agreement, and the typical percentage limit is 20%. However, in the event of a hostile takeover offer, it is useful to have the ability to issue authorized shares of common stock up to the 20% limit and even beyond that limit if the company is willing to violate its listing agreement.

Another useful antitakeover provision is to authorize for issuance shares of preferred stock whose terms and conditions can be established by the board, without shareholder approval. These shares of preferred stock are typically called "blank check" preferred stock. Preferred stock is useful in making acquisitions; this is particularly true of blank check preferred stock since the terms and conditions can be quickly established by the board of directors without shareholder approval. Blank check preferred stock is also useful in creating poison pills, which permit a board to deter a hostile takeover by creating a discriminatory dividend (which discriminates against the raider). Blank check preferred stock can also be given multiple voting rights, which is a useful attribute in deterring hostile takeovers. The issuance of preferred stock by the board of directors, without shareholder approval, is subject to the provisions of the listing agreement of the exchange on which the company's stock is traded, as noted.

TWO CLASSES OF STOCK

Although a classified board of directors is helpful protection against hedge funds and other activist shareholders, a patient and determined hedge fund still could obtain control over the board of directors over time.

The best antitakeover defense is having two classes of common stock. The first class of common stock, call it Class A common stock, is intended to be sold in the IPO and has the right to elect only a small percentage of the members of the board, or perhaps none at all. The second class of stock, call it Class B common stock, would elect a majority of the board of directors and, at the option of the holder, be convertible to Class A common stock, usually on a one-for-one basis. Both Class A and Class B stock are issued to the founder, with the majority of the shares being Class A stock. If stock options are granted, the options should be granted in the Class A stock to avoid dilution of control. Sometimes the Class A common stock is given a dividend preference to compensate for its lower voting power.

In the Martha Stewart Living Omnimedia, Inc. IPO, offered in October 1999, approximately $130 million of Class A common stock was sold to investors in a very successful public offering managed by Morgan Stanley Dean Witter (book manager). Each holder of Class A common stock was entitled to 1 vote per share. Martha Stewart continued to own all of Class B common stock, which was entitled to 10 votes per share. As a result, Martha Stewart had 96% of the total voting power after the IPO even though approximately 15% of the equity was sold in the IPO.

Comcast Corporation, currently a Standard & Poor's 500 company, had its IPO in 1972. It issued lower voting stock to the public in the IPO, retaining the higher voting stock for the founding Roberts family.

It is likely that lower voting stock will have to be sold at a discount to shares that have full voting rights. This discount is typically not more than 5%. Some underwriters refuse altogether to market an IPO with lower voting stock. Therefore, if the company elects to use two classes of stock, it may have to be very careful in the selection of an underwriter.

OTHER ANTITAKEOVER PROTECTIONS

The size of the board as well as the classification of the terms of the directors should be set forth in the charter, rather than in the by-laws, in order to prevent by-law amendments that change the size of the board. The charter should also state that any vacancy in the board, including those created by the removal of directors, should be filled exclusively by the vote of the remaining directors then in office, even if less than a quorum. The purpose of this provision is to prevent hedge funds and other activist shareholders from being able simultaneously to remove and replace directors.

Other antitakeover strategies can also be established in the charter. These include prohibiting action by shareholders by written consent, unless there has been prior approval by the board of directors for such consent. Hedge funds and other activist shareholders typically use consent solicitations to obtain voting power to change the board or the company's by-laws, without warning or the use of a proxy statement. Other antitakeover provisions include prohibiting removal of the board of directors except for cause, prohibiting shareholders from calling a special meeting, requiring a super-majority vote for removing directors with or without cause, allowing multiple director votes to the founders, and the like.

It is also useful to insert in the charter provisions requiring advance notice of nominations for directors (together with information about the nominee necessary for the proxy statement and the consent of such nominee) and advance notice of any proposals to be brought by shareholders at any shareholder meeting. It was reported that Sara Lee Corp. and Coach, Inc. amended their by-laws to require that any shareholder that nominates a director or makes another proposal must disclose whether it has "hedged its ownership" or has "any short position" in the stock. The purpose of these amendments is to ferret out hedge funds or other activist shareholders that make shareholder proposals and might not have the best interest of the company at heart because of their "short" position in the stock.[6]

Particularly valuable are clauses that prohibit purchase of more than a specified percentage (e.g., 10 %) of the company's stock without board permission and that permit the company to repurchase at a loss to the investor any excess shares acquired without board permission. Although these clauses have not been legally tested, their very appearance in the company's charter has a deterrent effect.

Most of these antitakeover clauses will not be acceptable to the IPO underwriter unless the IPO offering is very strong. Even if the potential underwriter objects to antitakeover clauses, almost none objects to changing the company's state of incorporation. Changing the company's state of incorporation to a state like Pennsylvania can dramatically increase the protection given to management from unwanted offers. Contrary to popular opinion, some states, including Delaware, may not be as protective against unfriendly suitors as other states.

No underwriter likes to have antitakeover clauses in the IPO. If the company's IPO is marginal, it is likely that few (if any) antitakeover clauses will survive underwriter scrutiny since they add unnecessary marketing problems.

If the company's IPO cannot be sold with major antitakeover clauses, then the company should consider installing such antitakeover clauses at the first annual shareholders' meeting after the company has gone public. In many states, the shareholder votes of the founders can be counted to approve antitakeover amendments to the charter. However, establishing two classes of stock is much more difficult, if not impossible, once the company has gone public.

When interviewing potential underwriters, the company should ask whether the existence of two classes of stock or other antitakeover clauses would prevent their underwriting the IPO. Many underwriters, in their eagerness to obtain business, are willing to accept reasonable antitakeover clauses if such provisions are contemplated at the time they are hired.

The next chapter discusses the necessity of establishing good corporate governance before the IPO.

NOTES

1. FactSet Research Systems, SharkRepellent.net.
2. Ibid.
3. Ibid.

4. A. Moore and S. Moffett, "Japan's Companies Gird for Attack," *Wall Street Journal*, April 30, 2008.

5. Thomas W. Briggs, "Corporate Governance and the New Hedge Fund Activism: An Empirical Analysis," *Journal of Corporation Law* (Summer 2007).

6. M. Andrejaczak, "UPDATE: Sara Lee, Coach Set Rules to Deter Devious Shareholders," *SmartMoney*, April 3, 2008.

Chapter 7

Develop Good Corporate Governance

Academic studies have shown that good corporate governance helps shareholder values.[1] Practicing good corporate governance will benefit a private company even if the company never has an initial public offering (IPO). This chapter discusses corporate governance structures that should be effectuated before an IPO.

SELECT THE COMPANY'S OWN INDEPENDENT BOARD MEMBERS

Consider appointing independent directors to the company's board prior to the IPO. Such independent directors can, if they have outstanding credentials, help establish the credibility of the management team to potential underwriters. They can also be helpful in introducing the company to potential underwriters and guiding the company through the IPO process.

Public companies are expected (and are required by SEC and stock exchange rules) to have an independent audit committee of their boards of directors. The underwriters will insist on independent directors in order to dress up the prospectus for the investment community.

The company will need independent directors anyway for its IPO. Therefore, why not obtain the benefit of their knowledge even before the IPO? Appointing them to the board before the IPO also gives the company a chance to evaluate them as directors. It may also forestall a request by the underwriters to have their own designees appointed to the board; however, this possibility is by no means assured. Even if the company never has an IPO, many private companies find that having independent directors on their board is helpful since they can give dispassionate advice regarding business operations.

Some potential directors prefer to be appointed to an advisory committee rather than to the board of directors, because of liability concerns. If the person has outstanding credentials and the company does not maintain liability insurance for directors and officers, it may wish to accommodate this request. However, it should be understood that the person will join the company board of directors when the IPO occurs since, presumably, the company will then purchase directors and officers liability insurance for them.

Most outside directors will accept a small stock option or other equity grant if the company does not wish to pay them in cash for their pre-IPO services.

WHO IS AN INDEPENDENT DIRECTOR?

The criteria for determining who is an independent director varies with the stock exchange rules on which the company will list its IPO. The definition of "independent directors" from the Nasdaq rules is as follows.

(a) For purposes of the Rule 4000 Series, unless the context requires otherwise:

(14) "Family Member" means a person's spouse, parents, children and siblings, whether by blood, marriage or adoption, or anyone residing in such person's home.

(15) "Independent director" means a person other than an executive officer or employee of the company or any other

individual having a relationship which, in the opinion of the issuer's board of directors, would interfere with the exercise of independent judgment in carrying out the responsibilities of a director. The following persons shall not be considered independent:

(A) a director who is, or at any time during the past three years was, employed by the company;

(B) a director who accepted or who has a Family Member who accepted any compensation from the company in excess of $120,000 during any period of twelve consecutive months within the three years preceding the determination of independence, other than the following:

  (i) compensation for board or board committee service;

  (ii) compensation paid to a Family Member who is an employee (other than an executive officer) of the company; or

  (iii) benefits under a tax-qualified retirement plan, or non-discretionary compensation.

Provided, however, that in addition to the requirements contained in this paragraph (B), audit committee members are also subject to additional, more stringent requirements under Rule 4350(d).

(C) a director who is a Family Member of an individual who is, or at any time during the past three years was, employed by the company as an executive officer;

(D) a director who is, or has a Family Member who is, a partner in, or a controlling shareholder or an executive officer of, any organization to which the company made, or from which the company received, payments for property or services in the current or any of the past three fiscal years that exceed 5% of the recipient's consolidated gross revenues for that year, or $200,000, whichever is more, other than the following:

  (i) payments arising solely from investments in the company's securities; or

  (ii) payments under non-discretionary charitable contribution matching programs.

(E) a director of the issuer who is, or has a Family Member who is, employed as an executive officer of another entity where at any time during the past three years any of the executive officers of the issuer serve on the compensation committee of such other entity; or

(F) a director who is, or has a Family Member who is, a current partner of the company's outside auditor, or was a partner or employee of the company's outside auditor who worked on the company's audit at any time during any of the past three years.

(G) omitted since applicable only to investment companies.

CHAIR OF THE BOARD[2]

BEST PRACTICE: Unless there is a lead or presiding director, the chair of the board should be an independent director, and independent directors should meet separately from management directors at least once a year. If the chair of the board is not an independent director, a lead or presiding director who is independent should be appointed.

The chair of the board is an important position and can establish the agenda for board meetings and the nature of board discussion. Unless there is a lead or presiding director, permitting the chief executive officer (CEO) to also be the chair of the board is a bad practice, since it permits the CEO to have too much power over the board of directors and undermines the board's fiduciary duty to monitor management. In situations in which the CEO or another management person is also the board chair, a lead or presiding independent director should be appointed. A Spencer Stuart survey of Standard & Poor 500 companies in mid-2005 indicated that 94% of companies with a combined chair and CEO position had a lead or presiding director.[3]

A lead or presiding director generally advises on board meeting schedules and agendas, chairs executive sessions of the board, oversees what information is provided to the board, leads the board in emergency situations, and generally serves as an intermediary between the board and management. Lead directors generally play a more influential and strategic role than presiding directors.[4]

Separate meetings of independent directors, at least yearly, permit these directors to have a free and frank discussion concerning management and the organization.

BOARD COMMITTEE STRUCTURE

> **BEST PRACTICE:** Directors of all organizations must establish audit committees, compensation committees, and, in appropriate cases, nominating/corporate governance committees composed entirely of independent directors or, alternatively, must perform the duties of such committees acting through the whole board of directors, which should consist of a majority of completely independent directors. All important committees of the board of directors should annually evaluate their own activities.

There are many duties imposed on the board of directors of any organization, and it may be preferable to divide these duties among committees of directors. These duties include selecting and monitoring the independent auditor, establishing compensation for at least the top management of the organization, having a committee that can nominate new directors, and monitoring the organization's corporate governance in order to establish an ethical, law-abiding culture that is necessary to avoid criminal prosecution as well as civil lawsuits.

If the board chooses to perform these functions as a whole, it may do so. However, in complex organizations, this can be very time consuming, and it is generally preferable to use a committee structure.

Annual self-evaluation of the functions of committees of the board is a best practice and is required by New York Stock Exchange rules for audit and compensation committees.

AUDIT COMMITTEE

> **BEST PRACTICE:** The audit committee must include persons who have the ability and willingness to fully understand the organization's accounting, and they must, at a minimum, hire and determine the compensation of the independent auditor, preapprove all auditing and nonauditing services performed by the independent auditor, and assure themselves of the independence of the auditing firm. The audit committee is responsible for overseeing the organization's financial reporting process and should understand and be familiar with the organization's system of internal controls.

The audit committee of the board of directors is probably the most important board committee, since it is responsible for supervising the organization's relationships with its outside auditors and overseeing the organization's financial reporting process, including reviewing its financial statements. The audit committee should be familiar with the organization's internal controls over financial reporting. The audit committee must consist of persons who have both the ability and the willingness to understand complex accounting concepts. To maintain the integrity of the audit process, the audit committee must hire and determine the compensation of the independent auditor and preapprove all audit and nonaudit services provided by the auditor.

If audited financial statements are obtained, the audit committee must determine the independence of the auditing firm.

The rules of Nasdaq and the Securities and Exchange Commission (SEC) require an audit committee consisting of at least three persons and require an audit committee to have at least one independent director on its committee at the time of its Nasdaq listing. Within 90 days of the IPO listing, a majority of the audit committee must be independent. Within one year of the IPO listing, all of the audit committee members must be independent, with a possible carve-out from the independence requirement for "exceptional and limited circum-stances" for one audit committee member.

Each Nasdaq company is required to certify that it has, and will continue to have, at least one member of the audit committee who has past employment experience in finance or accounting, requisite profes-sional certification in accounting, or any other comparable experience or background that results in the individual's financial sophistication, including being or having been a CEO, chief financial officer (CFO), or other senior officer with financial oversight responsibilities.[5]

COMPENSATION COMMITTEE

BEST PRACTICE: The compensation committee's responsibili-ties should include overseeing the organization's overall compen-sation structure, policies, and programs (including board compensation); establishing or recommending to the board per-formance goals and objectives for the CEO and other members of senior management; and establishing or recommending to the in-dependent directors compensation for the CEO and senior management.

In the corporate governance structure, the compensation committee is as important as the audit committee. Since the culture of an organ-ization is reflective of its compensation policies, the policies adopted by the compensation committee can be instrumental in establishing an ethical, law-abiding culture.

Unfortunately, many compensation committees limit their activities to the compensation of the top executives only. This is a mistake un-less some other committee (e.g., corporate governance committee) has been assigned this duty. The compensation committee (or possibly the corporate governance committee) must study the entire compensation system within the organization to determine whether the incentives and disincentives are consistent with an ethical, law-abiding culture.

WHISTLEBLOWER POLICY

BEST PRACTICE: A whistleblower policy should be established for all organizations (except to the extent prohibited by certain foreign laws) since, according to a 2008 survey by the Association of Certified Fraud Examiners,[6] fraud is detected 57.7% of the time by tips.

Whether the organization is public, private, or not for profit, it is important for the board of directors or one of its committees to make itself accessible to employees by establishing a whistleblower policy that permits employees to confidentially communicate with the board or its audit committee. Proper handling of employee complaints helps to avoid lawsuits (including class actions) and government investigations. A whistleblower policy is required by the Sarbanes-Oxley Act of 2002 (SOX).

INTERNAL CONTROLS

It is important for the company to establish good internal controls prior to the IPO. In a U.S. IPO, the internal control provisions of SOX will become applicable upon the filing of an IPO registration statement under the 1933 Act. On or about the effective date of the IPO registration statement, the accounting provisions of the Foreign Corrupt Practices Act of 1977, previously discussed, will become applicable. The CEO and CFO of the company will, shortly after the IPO effective date, have to certify in periodic filings with the SEC as to the adequacy of its internal controls.

Therefore, it makes sense to attempt to establish good internal controls well before the IPO target date. Although the independent auditor will not have to attest as to the adequacy of these controls until at least a year after the IPO, the personal liability of the CEO and CFO with respect to their certifications should induce the company to establish internal controls well before the IPO target date.

ENTERPRISE RISK MANAGEMENT

> **BEST PRACTICE:** Directors must either directly or through committees identify the major risks of an organization, prioritize those risks, and establish internal controls and a compliance program to help ameliorate such risks. The major risk analysis should be used to develop a committee structure within the board of directors, with each committee having an oversight role with respect to each major risk.

It is important to identify and prioritize the major risks of an organization and establish internal controls to help ameliorate these risks. The board or one of its committees should, with the assistance of management, legal counsel, and independent accountants, perform such an analysis and establish appropriate internal controls. Board committee structure should be established with a view to having a committee with oversight of each major risk.

Performing this risk analysis will assist the board in demonstrating that it has complied with its fiduciary duties. The Delaware Chancery Court has held in the *Caremark* case[7] that one of the board's fiduciary duties is to implement a compliance program to prevent violations of the law. The court also stated that a director's duties include "an attempt in good faith to assure that a corporate information reporting system, which the Board concludes is adequate exist."

No system for identifying risks is perfect. Likewise, no one-size-fits-all analysis is possible. Each organization has peculiar risks that must be identified and prioritized. A multiplicity of civil and criminal statutes, rules, and regulations (federal, state, and local) require that experienced legal counsel be used to assist in this risk analysis. At a minimum, every director should be generally aware of the more significant federal, state, and local statutes applicable to the business of the organization.

A good source for organizational risk identification is to review the problems that have previously occurred in the organization or in other similar organizations. Directors should require an industry report at each board meeting that not only reviews the status of competitors but discusses any government investigation or any regulatory or other legal issues that are affecting organizations in the same industry. If another company in the industry has disclosed a government investigation, directors should inquire as to whether the practices being investigated are also being practiced by the organization. If the organization is engaged in the same practice or does something similar, it is likely that the organization will be dragged into the government investigation of the other company in the industry.

Some risks are insurable; therefore, any risk analysis must include an analysis of existing insurance coverages.

One method of analyzing risk is by using balance sheet accounts and rating the various risks that can affect these accounts. Many other methods of analyzing risks should also be considered.

Once the major risks have been identified, the board and management should develop methods to attempt to control these risks. Although no risk control system is perfect, the attempt to analyze and control risks will help the organization to comply with the U.S. Department of Justice Sentencing Guidelines. Compliance with these guidelines helps to protect the organization from criminal indictment and fines.

Chapter 8 deals with the important topic of creating bail-out opportunities and taking advantage of IPO windows prior to the IPO.

NOTES

1. Lawrence D. Brown and Marcus L. Caylor, "Corporate Governance and Firm Performance," Georgia State University, December 7, 2004. See also Igor Filatotchev, "Gong Public with Good Governance: Board Selection

and Share Ownership in UK IPO Firms," Bradford University School of Management, April 2002.

2. Selected "best practices" from *Corporate Governance Best Practices,* Frederick D. Lipman and L. Keith Lipman (John Wiley & Sons, 2006), which should be considered by private companies that are planning an IPO.

3. "A Closer Look at Lead or Presiding Directors," Spencer Stuart, Cornerstone of the Board, The New Governance Committee, Vol. 1, Issue 4 (2006).

4. Ibid., p. 9.

5. Although Nasdaq does not require an audit committee to have a member who qualifies as an "audit committee financial expert," a person qualifying as such (as defined in Item 407(d)(5) of Regulation S-K) is presumed to have the requisite financial sophistication.

6. 2008 Report to the Nation on Occupational Fraud & Abuse, Association of Certified Fraud Examiners (ACFE), www.ACFE.com.

7. *Caremark International, Inc. Derivative Litigation,* Docket No. 1996 WL 549894, Delaware Chancery Court.

Create Insider Bail-Out Opportunities and Take Advantage of IPO Windows

It is common to speak about an initial public offering (IPO) as an "exit" event. In reality, IPOs merely pave the way for an exit event by the shareholders of the private company.

Underwriters of IPOs are very wary of permitting shareholders of a private company to sell any significant amount of their stock in the IPO. It looks like a bail-out. Typically, the underwriters will require a lock-up of the stock of the public company owned by the shareholders of the former private company. The lock-up period typically extends for three to six months, but a number of lock-up provisions permit an earlier release of the shares if certain stock price goals are achieved after the IPO. Lock-up periods, however, can be much longer than six months in certain kinds of very risky IPOs.

In view of the likelihood that the IPO will not produce any liquidity for shareholders of the private company, it is useful to structure the private company in a manner that permits some liquidity to result from the IPO.

This chapter initially discusses methods of structuring the company to permit private company shareholders to gain some amount of liquidity from the IPO. A discussion of the importance of IPO windows follows.

SUBCHAPTER S AND OTHER TAX FLOW-THROUGH ENTITIES

A Subchapter S corporation, a limited liability company, or other tax flow-through entity creates unique bail-out opportunities. A Subchapter S corporation is a corporation that has elected to be taxed pursuant to Subchapter S of the Internal Revenue Code of 1986 (as amended). The shareholders of a Subchapter S corporation are personally taxed on the corporation's income for federal income tax purposes. The same tax rules are true for equity holders of limited liability companies, limited partnerships, and other tax flow-through entities.

Underwriters typically do not object to the withdrawal of this previously taxed income from the corporation or other entity upon the closing of the IPO. Of course, the company still must be reasonably funded after the withdrawal.

The withdrawal is in reality a dividend to insiders. It is typically justified by the fact that the income was previously taxed to the shareholders or other equity holders.

Shareholders of non–Subchapter S corporations (so-called C or regular business corporations) have much greater difficulty convincing underwriters to permit a dividend on the eve of an IPO. Yet, economically, such dividends are very similar to a Subchapter S withdrawal.

For example, in the 1996 IPO by Donna Karan International, the company raised approximately $242 million of which $116 million was paid to Donna Karan and her partners personally in satisfaction of promissory notes representing their previously taxed undistributed income. The $116 million was received from the IPO even though no shares were sold in the IPO by either Donna Karan or her partners.

If all of the company's assets are not needed in its business, consider transferring the excess assets to the founder and other shareholders, keeping only the core assets in the business. These pre-IPO transfers to the founders and other shareholders create an indirect bail-out.

Even non–tax flow-through entities have been successful in structuring their IPOs with dividends. An example would be the 2006 IPO of Chart Industries, Inc. The company raised $175.3 million, after deducting underwriting discounts, and used $150.3 million to pay a dividend to its stockholders existing immediately prior to the IPO and to certain management members.

OTHER INSIDER BAIL-OUT OPPORTUNITIES

Underwriters are less concerned with the company using part of the proceeds of the IPO to pay debts or other obligations to an insider or to a bank or an institutional lender that funded an insider transaction, provided the debts or other obligations were incurred in a legitimate transaction.

For example, the insider may enter into a long-term patent license or real estate lease with the company and use a portion of the IPO proceeds to fund the license or lease payments. Likewise, the insider may sell property to the company, provided it is normally used in company operations. Alternatively, if payments to the insider as a result of the license, lease, or sale were originally funded with bank debt, underwriters generally do not object to the repayment of the bank debt with the IPO proceeds. This may be true even if the insider is a personal guarantor of the bank debt.

However, the sale of insider stock to the company on the eve of the IPO would raise eyebrows unless the sale resulted from the retirement or death of one of the company's founders.

A private company could also leverage itself with bank or other institutional debt prior to the IPO, use the proceeds from the debt to pay a dividend to its shareholders, and repay the debt from the net proceeds of the IPO. This transaction is sometimes called a *leveraged recapitalization.* So long as the bank or other institutional debt is not personally guaranteed by the shareholders, this is an excellent method of withdrawing equity from the company prior to the IPO, using IPO proceeds to extinguish the debt.

Obviously, if the debts or other obligations to the insider or to a bank or other institutional lender are incurred on the eve of the IPO, it looks more like a disguised bail-out. Therefore, any insider transaction should generally happen well before the IPO. Under Item 504 of Securities and Exchange Commission (SEC) Regulation S-K, if the indebtedness of the company to the insider was incurred within one year, disclosure would be required of the use of the proceeds of this indebtedness.

Once the private company is leveraged with debt either to an insider or to a bank or other institutional lender, the shareholders of the private company should consider making gifts and doing other estate planning. The debt reduces the value of the stock of the private company and therefore facilitates gift and estate tax planning.

TAKING ADVANTAGE OF IPO WINDOWS

IPO windows open and close quickly.[1] The company's short-term planning should take advantage of these windows. The company may prefer to have its IPO in six months or a year. However, in six months or a year there may be no market for IPOs. The company's plans must be flexible enough to take advantage of the windows that exist.

Exhibit 8.1 shows the great variation in the number of firm-commitment IPO underwritings from year to year that are declared effective by the SEC.

Fads often develop in IPOs when investor interest is high. For example, in 2008, oil and gas equipment and service companies are expected to be hot; Internet issues were popular in the late 1990s; previously, environmental and biotechnology issues were popular, but currently they are not. If the company has a product line that can fit

Exhibit 8.1 Initial Public Offerings, 1970–2007: The IPO Long View

	No. IPOs	Aggregate IPO Offer (in millions)
1970	138	$584
1971	253	$1,072
1972	495	$2,201
1973	95	$1,431
1974	9	$99
1975	6	$189
1976	40	$337
1977	32	$222
1978	38	$225
1979	62	$398
1980	149	$1,387
1981	348	$3,115
1982	122	$1,339
1983	685	$12,461
1984	357	$3,869
1985	310	$7,619
1986	726	$22,246
1987	548	$23,472
1988	288	$23,472
1989	251	$13,277
1990	213	$10,055
1991	400	$24,610
1992	597	$37,934
1993	808	$56,148
1994	631	$32,524
1995	570	$29,536
1996	853	$51,325
1997	615	$44,900
1998	370	$44,791
1999	541	$85,720
2000	446	$105,770
2001	99	$42,652
2002	92	$27,572
2003	87	$17,699

(Continued)

Exhibit 8.1   (Continued)

	No. IPOs	Aggregate IPO Offer (in millions)
2004	253	$46,824
2005	234	$36,833
2006	246	$45,642
2007	282	$60,596

Source: Information provided by www.IPOVitalSigns.com, a product of CCH, a Walters Kluwer business.

within a fad, the company may want to change its IPO target date to take advantage of it.

The history of IPO fads is that the highest valuations are given to the companies that have the earliest IPOs. Ultimately, the supply of companies feeding the fad increases and begins to overwhelm investor demand. This results in lower valuations for the later fad companies. The history of Internet IPOs followed this same trend. The moral is that the early bird catches the worm.

Particular attention should be paid to IPOs of other companies in the company's industry. If another company in the same business recently had a successful IPO, underwriters will be eager to market the company's public issue. This is particularly true if the current market price of the stock of the similar company is above its IPO price. The company's stock will be attractive to underwriters since they can market the company's IPO to potential investors with the analogy of the prior successful IPO.

This concludes the pre-IPO planning opportunities. In Chapter 9 we turn to structuring an international IPO.

NOTES

1. See paper by M. Lowry and G. Schwert, "IPO Market Cycles: Bubbles or Sequential Learning?" University of Rochester, William E. Simon Graduate School of Business Administration, revised June 2001.

Part Two
International IPOs

Structuring an International IPO

Many initial public offerings (IPOs) today are international with multiple listings on exchanges throughout the world. The purpose of this chapter is to guide U.S. companies in effectuating an international IPO without having to comply with registration provisions of the Securities Exchange Act of 1934 (1934 Act) or most of the provisions of the Sarbanes-Oxley Act (SOX).

There are four primary reasons for a U.S. company to have an international offering:

1. To avoid the application of some of the more onerous provisions of SOX, particularly the expensive attestation report on internal controls from the independent auditor required under Section 404 of SOX

2. To avoid the restrictive requirements of U.S. generally accepted accounting principles (GAAP) accounting, which significantly increase accounting and auditing costs

3. To avoid the expense of having more than one or two independent directors on the board

4. To avoid the expensive and burdensome Securities and Exchange
Commission (SEC) reporting requirements

SELECTING AN INTERNATIONAL EXCHANGE
FOR AN IPO

There are a number of factors to be considered in selecting an international exchange for an IPO. These include:

- Does the company have any connection with the country in which
  that exchange is located? This is not a crucial factor, but it is helpful to the IPO marketing to have some relationship with the country. The Alternate Investment Market (AIM) of the London Stock
  Exchange and many other international exchanges do not require
  any contact with the country for an IPO listing.

- Are there prestigious underwriters available in the country to sponsor an IPO on that international exchange of the dollar size intended? Studies have shown that prestigious IPO underwriters are
  more likely to have successful IPOs with a lower amount of underpricing.[1] Many international stock exchanges will permit very
  small IPOs, unlike the major U.S. stock exchanges. For example,
  the junior board of the Toronto Stock Exchange, called the TSX
  Venture Exchange, will support companies in the early stage of
  development.

- What is the likely level of underwriter discount and IPO underpricing? For example, IPO underpricing is severe in China, according
  to at least one academic study.[2]

- Has the country adopted burdensome SOX requirements? Many
  countries have adopted some variations of SOX, but typically they
  have not adopted the requirement for an independent auditor's attestation report on internal controls under Section 404, which has
  been the primary criticism of SOX. For example, the Canadian Securities Administrators have adopted what has been christened

"Canadian SOX" but have refused to require an opinion of the independent auditor on internal controls.

- What kind of after-market support is available from the underwriter?
- What are the likely out-of-pocket expenses for effectuating the IPO and to comply with post-IPO disclosure requirements?
- What is the likely lockup period for insider stock? This varies from country to country and from underwriter to underwriter.

Many other factors should be considered, such as the ability to effectuate follow-on offerings, any currency convertibility risks, the litigation atmosphere in the country, and others.

Each country has its own peculiarities. In the United States, pre-IPO trading (or gray market trading) in IPO shares is prohibited. Most European countries, however, have a gray market for IPOs mostly organized by independent brokers, where investors can speculate on future stock prices of companies that are in the process of going public.[3] Allegedly, lawsuits against "IPO firms" are not possible in India.[4] It is not unusual in countries with less developed capital markets to have "daily volatility limits" restricting price fluctuations in the post-IPO market, such as occurred on the Athens Stock Exchange during the 1990s. On the Kuala Lumpur Stock Exchange, it is quite common for major shareholders to have a three-year lockup. From 1996 to 1999, Malaysia required a profit guarantee from the major shareholders to the public shareholders as an alternative to a three-year lockup.[5]

AVOIDING SOX*

The SEC has made it difficult for companies incorporated in the United States to avoid SOX if they have an international IPO. Any U.S.-incorporated company that has more than 500 shareholders of record[6]*worldwide* and more than $10 million of assets (measured as of the end of its most recent fiscal year) is required to register under

---

*Co-authored by Jeffrey M. Taylor, Esq, Philadelphia office, Blank Rome, LLP.

Section 12 of the 1934 Act, and this registration (among other things) triggers compliance with SOX. Thus, if a Delaware corporation had 501 British citizens as record shareholders and more than $10 million of assets (measured as of the end of its most recent fiscal year), the Delaware corporation would have to register its stock under Section 12 of the 1934 Act, even though it had no U.S. citizens or residents as shareholders.

SOX is also triggered if a company (whether U.S. incorporated or otherwise) either (a) files a registration statement with the SEC under the 1933 Act (e.g., to raise capital), regardless of the number of world-wide shareholders of record or (b) listed stock for trading on the New York Stock Exchange (NYSE), Nasdaq, or any other U.S. national se-curities exchange. Even the OTC Bulletin Board requires that all listed companies be required to file reports under section 13 or 15(d) of the 1934 Act, thereby triggering SOX compliance. The only "market" in the United States that does not automatically trigger SOX compliance is the Pink Sheets, as will be discussed.

Therefore, if the primary purpose of the international IPO is to avoid the application of the 1934 Act and SOX, a foreign holding company must be formed that does not file a registration statement under the 1933 Act (excluding registration statements solely to regis-ter American Depositary Receipts on Form F-6), and, if it has any trading in its securities in the United States, the trading must occur solely on the Pink Sheets (discussed in the next section). This foreign holding company typically would be formed in the British Virgin Islands or the Cayman Islands, but other friendly foreign countries are also available.

The shareholders of the U.S. company would, simultaneously with the closing of the international IPO, transfer their shares in the U.S. company to the foreign holding company. In return, the U.S. share-holders would receive either shares of the foreign holding company or, more typically, American Depositary Receipts (ADRs) indirectly representing such shares. This assumes that the issuance of the shares or ADRs by the foreign holding company to the U.S. shareholders of the private company would not trigger a registration statement under the 1933 Act (excluding a registration statement solely with respect to ADRs on Form F-6) because of an available private placement or similar exemption from the registration provisions of the 1933 Act.

The transfer of the shares of the U.S. company to the foreign holding company would be taxable under U.S. federal income tax laws unless certain requirements were satisfied. These tax requirements are specified in Chapter 10 of this book. In general, after the international IPO, the U.S. shareholders would have to own less than 50% of the value and voting power of the shares of the foreign holding company in order to avoid certain adverse U.S. federal income tax effects. See Chapter 10 for more details.

In order to avoid SOX and 1934 Act compliance after the international IPO, the foreign holding company would have to qualify as a "foreign private issuer" and satisfy one of the two exemptions described in the next section. This assumes that after the international IPO, the company will have more than 500 shareholders of record worldwide and more than $10 million in assets at the end of a fiscal year. Since it is unlikely that any company will, after completing an international IPO, have assets of less than $10 million at the end of its fiscal year, we assume for the rest of this chapter that the less–than–$10 million exclusion does not apply.

FOREIGN PRIVATE ISSUER

In order to be a foreign private issuer, an issuer must first be "a corporation or other organization incorporated or organized under the laws of any foreign country."[7] In addition, the issuer must satisfy *either* of these two tests:

Test #1: At least 50% of the issuer's outstanding voting securities must be directly or indirectly held by non-U.S. residents.

   or

Test #2: *All* of these four points must be satisfied:

1. At least 50% of the issuer's executive officers must be both non-U.S. *citizens* and non-U.S. *residents*.

2. At least 50% of the issuer's directors (or other persons providing similar functions) must be both non-U.S. *citizens* and non-U.S. *residents*.

3. At least 50% of the assets of the issuer must be located outside the United States.

4. The business of the issuer must be administered principally outside of the United States.[8]

Thus, the foreign holding company would be considered a "foreign private issuer" so long as less than 50% of the outstanding voting securities were held by non-U.S. residents. As discussed in Chapter 10, the transfer of the stock of the U.S. company to the foreign holding company could be subject to adverse U.S. federal income tax consequences unless U.S. taxpayers, after the international IPO, owned less than 50% of both the value and voting power the shares (or ADRs) of the foreign holding company. Thus, the federal income tax considerations dovetail with the desire to qualify the foreign holding company as a foreign private issuer.

Assuming that the foreign holding company was considered a foreign private issuer with more than 500 shareholders worldwide, the foreign holding company could avoid registration under the 1934 Act and thereby avoid SOX applicability if it satisfied *either one* of these two conditions:

• The foreign holding company could not, after the international IPO, have more than 300 holders of record of such class who are U.S. residents as of the end of its most recently completed fiscal year.[9] Securities held of record by a broker, dealer, bank, or nominee for any of them for the accounts of customers resident in the United States must be counted as held in the United States by the number of separate accounts for which the securities are held. Therefore, great care must be taken in the international IPO to obtain representations of non-U.S. residency from the IPO investors and to prevent them from reselling or otherwise transferring the securities to U.S. residents through restrictions on the stock certificates and in the charter.

- The company must (a) maintain a listing of the class of securities on one or more exchanges in one or two non-U.S. jurisdictions comprising its primary trading market (accounting for at least 55% of the trading worldwide in the class of securities during its most recently completed fiscal year)[9], (b) satisfy certain electronic publishing requirements in English on its Web site or otherwise[10] and (c) not be required to file or furnish SEC reports under Section 13(a) or 15(d) of the 1934 Act.

After an international IPO, the ADRs representing shares of the foreign holding company could be quoted in the United States through the Pink Sheets without triggering any registration requirement under the 1934 Act. The Pink Sheets is a broker-dealer quotation system that allows quotations to be published and accessed through the Internet and other electronic and written media. A U.S. broker-dealer would have to apply to list the ADRs for trading on the Pink Sheets.[11] To permit U.S. broker-dealers to trade on the Pink Sheets, the company would have to supply to the broker-dealer financial and other information specified in Rule 15c2-11 of the 1934 Act. This information is easy to prepare and not burdensome. The trading price of the securities on the Pink Sheets is available through the Internet.

IPOS ON AIM[12]

One of the more flexible international exchanges for an IPO is the Alternate Investment Market of the London Stock Exchange. The London Stock Exchange is divided into the Main Market for larger companies and AIM for smaller growing companies. The London Stock Exchange does not consider the securities admitted to AIM to be admitted to a regulated market. The Main Market is the exchange's regulated market for larger companies and must meet European Union

(EU) Directives. The United Kingdom's law on public offers of securities is governed by the Prospectus Rules published by the Financial Services Authority.[13]

The advantages of an AIM offering are discussed next.

- The London Stock Exchange does not impose any minimum requirement for a market capitalization, trading record, share price, or shares in public hands (or free float), and the exchange does not have the decision as to whether a company is suitable for admission to AIM—this responsibility is placed on the *nominated advisor* (Nomad). A list of Nomads is contained on the Web site of the London Stock Exchange.[14]

- The role of the Nomad is to judge whether the company is appropriate for the AIM market, to explain the AIM rules to the company's board of directors, and to insure that they are aware of their responsibilities and obligations.

- The London Stock Exchange has not adopted many of the more onerous provisions of SOX and does not have any requirements for an auditor attestation report of internal controls.

- The London Stock Exchange requires financial reports to use the more flexible international accounting standards rather than U.S. GAAP.

- There is no requirement for quarterly financial reports (such as Form 10-Q). Only semiannual reports are required, and these are not as burdensome in their content as the Form 10-Q.

- The reporting requirements are in general much less burdensome than those of the SEC.

For example, once a company is admitted to trading on AIM, it is subject to certain continuing obligations, including producing and filing annual financial statements, within six months after the year-end, prepared in accordance with International Accounting Standards. This contrasts favorably with SEC rules that require an annual report on Form 10-K to be filed within a period that can be as little as 60 days after the end of the fiscal year. Even the half-yearly reports required for AIM companies need only be filed within three months of the end of the half-year. In contrast, Form 10-Q must be filed with the SEC within 45 days after the end of each quarter.

Other continuing obligations of an AIM company include these, which are similar to obligations imposed on U.S. companies (except for the Nomad and broker) but are nowhere near as burdensome:

- Retaining a nominated advisor and broker
- Publishing price-sensitive information and other stipulated information without delay
- Publishing details of any transactions with related parties, other than those that fall below a 5% class test, without delay
- Imposing a code on share dealing for directors and applicable employees
- Where an acquisition would result in a reverse takeover, obtaining shareholder approval and producing a new admission document
- Where a disposal would result in a fundamental change of business, obtaining shareholder approval
- Ensuring that the securities admitted to trading on AIM remain freely transferable and eligible for electronic settlement

There are several disadvantages of an AIM IPO for a U.S. company. First, the company must have a Nomad sponsor the IPO. If no Nomads are interested in the company, it will not be able to have an AIM IPO. Second, the AIM market is primarily an institutional market rather than a retail market, which typically means that the company may have a somewhat lower IPO valuation and the market will not be as liquid because of the absence of retail investors. It has been reported that the AIM is characterized by wide spreads between the bid and asked prices for the listed stocks, primarily because there is only one market maker.[15] This significant spread is also true of stocks traded on the U.S. OTC Bulletin Board and Pink Sheets.

It has also been reported that the investment statements of a number of U.K. institutional investors bar them from investing in AIM
companies, primarily because of a number of high-profile frauds and
failures on AIM.[16]

SEC commissioner Roel Campos allegedly uttered some impolitic
words about the London Stock Exchange's AIM in front of a reporter
from Dow Jones Newswire, to wit: "I'm concerned that 30 percent of
issuers that list on AIM are gone in a year. That feels like a casino to me
and I believe that investors will treat it as such."[17] This produced a storm
of criticism in the British press with the AIM responding in this way:
"The failure rate is more like 3 percent. Further, U.S. companies
have been flocking to AIM, almost doubling since 2006 to 60."[18] One
subsequent British academic study aptly titled "Is AIM a Casino?"
concluded:

> The short-run results show that AIM IPOs have high probability of sur-
> vival post-IPO. . . . The long-run results show that the survival time of
> the IPOs increase with age and size of the firms, while the initial re-
> turns have no impact on the survival time of the IPO firms.[19]

The AIM section of the London Stock Exchange does not require a
shareholders' advisory vote on executive compensation. The Directors' Remuneration Report, which requires a shareholders' advisory
under the U.K. Companies Acts, does not apply to AIM-listed securities as such. It applies to securities listed on the Official List maintained by the U.K. Listing Authority and to securities officially listed
in another European Economic Area (EEA) state and to securities admitted to dealing on the NYSE and on Nasdaq.

Other persons, in addition to the Nomad, who have a role in an
AIM IPO are:

- The broker, which is a securities house and member of the London
  Stock Exchange and is responsible for the fundraising
- The legal advisor, which oversees due diligence on behalf of the
  Nomad, changes to directors contracts, and verification of the

statements in the admission document, and provides ongoing advice on legal obligations

- The reporting accountant, who conducts an independent review of the company's financial records and assists in preparing financial information required to be published

- A public/investor relations advisor, at the company's election, to assist the company in managing information concerning the IPO

UNDERPRICING ON AIM

One study has indicated that IPOs listed on AIM "appear to be only conservatively mispriced when contrasted to main board IPO listings in the US, UK and other countries."[20] There is not significant IPO underpricing on AIM as opposed to the Main Board. That study also indicated that there was more underpricing in the U.S. markets than in the AIM market for comparable companies.

GROWTH OF AIM

The statistics in Exhibit 9.1 show the significant growth of the AIM market since its founding in 1995.

EQUITY MARKET VALUE OF AIM COMPANIES

Exhibit 9.2 provides information regarding the equity market value of the companies on the AIM as of February 2008.[21] Note that the largest percentage of AIM-listed companies have a market value of less than $12 million in U.S. dollars.

Exhibit 9.1 AIM Market Growth

	No. Companies			Market Value (£m)	No. Admissions			Money Raised £m		
	UK*	International	Total		UK	International	Total	New	Further	Total
6/19/1995	10	0	10	82.2						
1995	118	3	121	2,382.4	120	3	123	69.5	25.3	94.8
1996	235	17	252	5,298.5	131	14	145	514.1	302.3	816.4
1997	286	22	308	5,655.1	100	7	107	344.1	350.2	694.3
1998	291	21	312	4,437.9	68	7	75	267.5	290.1	557.6
1999	325	22	347	13,468.5	96	6	102	333.7	599.8	933.5
2000	493	31	524	14,935.2	265	12	277	1,754.1	1,319.7	3,073.8
2001	587	42	629	11,607.2	162	15	177	593.1	535.3	1,128.4
2002	654	50	704	10,252.3	147	13	160	490.1	485.8	975.8
2003	694	60	754	18,358.5	146	16	162	1,095.4	999.7	2,095.2
2004	905	116	1021	31,753.4	294	61	355	2,775.9	1,880.2	4,656.1
2005	1,179	220	1,399	56,618.5	399	120	519	6,461.2	2,481.2	8,942.4
2006	1,330	304	1,634	94,364.0	338	124	462	9,943.8	5,734.3	15,678.1
2007	1,347	347	1,694	97,561.0	197	87	284	6,581.1	9,602.8	16,183.9
2008 to Feb	**1,337**	**346**	**1,683**	**93,619.1**	**17**	**4**	**21**	**212.3**	**678.6**	**891.0**
Launch to date					**2,480**	**489**	**2,969**	**31,435.9**	**25,285.4**	**56,721.3**

*One pound (£) equals U.S. $1.98 as of April 30, 2008.

Exhibit 9.2 Equity Market Value of AIM Companies

Market Value Range (£m)	No. Companies	%	Equity Market Value (£m)	%
	AIM (UK & International)			
Over 2,000	1	0.1	2,095.2	2.2
1,000–2,000	1	0.1	1,138.3	1.2
500–1,000	18	1.1	11,767.4	12.6
250–500	56	3.3	18,325.7	19.6
100–250	180	10.7	27,684.9	29.6
50–100	218	13.0	15,062.5	16.1
25–50	255	15.2	8,988.0	9.6
10–25	355	21.1	5,991.6	6.4
5–10	233	13.9	1,727.0	1.8
2–5	198	11.8	688.0	0.7
0–2	140	8.3	150.4	0.2
Unvalued securities	0	0.0	-	-
Suspended	27	1.6	-	-
Totals	**1,682**	**100.0**	**93,619.1**	**100.0**
More than £50m	474	28.2	76,074.0	81.3
Less than £50m	1,181	70.2	17,545.1	18.7
Less than £25m	926	55.1	8,557.1	9.1

COMPARISON OF IPO COSTS ON NASDAQ AND AIM

Exhibits 9.3 and 9.4 show a June 2006 comparison by Canaccord Adams Limited, an AIM Nomad, of IPO costs on Nasdaq and AIM.[22]

However, as noted in Chapter 1, the legal and accounting expenses quoted in 2007 for AIM offerings are estimated at $400,000 to $1 million each, as a result of the devaluation of the U.S. dollar.[23] Therefore, AIM expenses do not differ significantly from U.S. legal and accounting expenses.

OTHER EUROPEAN EXCHANGES

A survey of the European IPO market indicated that on every stock exchange there is generally a "Main Market" designed for listing

Exhibit 9.3   IPO Costs on Nasdaq and AIM

	Nasdaq (in U.S. $)	AIM (in U.S. $)
Shares issued (number)	5m	20m
Amount raised	50m	50m
Registration fee	c.9,000	c.20,000
Filing fee	c.9,000	na
Listing fee	c.100,000	c.7,500
Printing	c,220,000	c.40,000
Legal fees	c.750,000	c.600,000
Accounting fees	c.490,000	c.350,000
Blue sky fees	c.10,000	na
Transfer agent, registrar fees	c.10,000	c.14,000
Retainer	na	c.275,000
Underwriting discount/step-up	c.3,500,000	c.2,500,000
Miscellaneous	c.75,000	c.50,000
Total approximate cost	**c.5,713,000**	**c.3,856,500**

Exhibit 9.4   Annual Costs of Being a $200 Million Public Company

	Nasdaq (in U.S. $)	AIM (in U.S. $
Directors' and officers' insurance	c.500,000	c.100,000
Directors' fees and expenses	c.150,000	c.150,000
Annual audit fees	c.300,000	c.150,000
404 compliance	c.500,000	na
Legal fees	c.300,000	c.300,000
Internal costs for SEC and exchange compliance	c.300,000	na
SEC filing expenses and listing fees	c.35,000	c.7,000
Nomad expenses	na	c.90,000
Other (investor relations, mailing, etc.)	c.250,000	c.125,000
Total approximate cost	**c.2,335,000**	**c.922,000**

large companies, a parallel market that caters to middle and small cap-
italizations, and a "New Market" that caters to growth companies.
There are exceptions to this rule, such as the Stockholm stock exchange (OMX, Sweden), the Vienna stock exchange (VSE, Austria),
and the Warsaw stock exchange (WSE, Poland), all of which never
opened a New Market, and the Swiss exchange (SWX) and Deutsch
Börse, which closed their New Markets.[24] The survey states:

> Parallel or second markets generally have the lowest listing require-
> ments. On many of these markets, no minimum market capitalization
> is necessary to be listed, and if there is a minimum, the value is about
> EUR one million,[25] the only exception being Euronext Paris with the
> highest requirement in the range of EUR 12–15 million. The minimum
> percentage of *shares to be offered to the public* generally equals *10%*
> and reaches 20% in a few cases (Greece, Spain and Switzerland). In
> terms of accounting track records, typically, *financial statements* must
> be provided over a period of *two years prior to the IPO*, implying a
> minimum period of existence of two years for the issuing firm. . . . New
> markets usually cater to young high-growth companies, which implies
> that listing is not authorized solely on the basis of historical data but
> can be justified by growth prospects. For that reason, listing on a New
> Market never requires more than *one year of accounting records* but
> always involves raising funds, with a *capital increase representing at
> least 50%* of the shares offered to the public. Listing standards on New
> Markets often focus on disclosure and governance. . ., and generally re-
> quire periodic audited financial statements meeting international ac-
> counting standards. Concerning size, the requirements are not expressed
> in terms of market capitalization but in terms of shareholders' equity
> with a *minimum requested book value of between one and five million
> euros*. At least *20% of the shares must be distributed to the public* (30%
> for the Nuovo Mercato in Italy and 15% for the NM list in Finland).[26]

The success of the AIM in attracting IPOs, as opposed to other
European stock exchanges, is that it is not limited to so-called new
economy companies; does not require any minimum equity size, capitalization, or age; and does not impose lockup periods, although the
Nomad may require a lockup.

HONG KONG STOCK EXCHANGE*

The Hong Kong Stock Exchange, like the London Stock Exchange, is divided into two boards, the "Main Board" and the Growth Enterprise Market (GEM). The GEM may be considered the Hong Kong analog to the AIM.

GEM was launched in November 1999 with the aim to provide a platform for relatively new and emerging businesses to obtain a listing and raise capital. It is suitable for enterprises that may not be able to fulfill the profitability/profit track record requirements and therefore are not eligible to be listed on the Main Board.

This alternative market is very much viewed as a second board, and can be used as a stepping-stone to the Main Board. Companies listed on GEM are typically dynamic young companies with big growth potential, but the risk for investors is higher, as many of the companies lack a profit track record. The GEM is therefore viewed as a "high growth, high risk" and more volatile *caveat emptor* market for informed, professional, and institutional investors. The attractiveness of GEM has, however, cooled somewhat over the past few years, with the number of companies being listed decreasing.

GEM LISTING REQUIREMENTS

GEM has its own set of listing rules, but shares the same listing committee with the Main Board. A main characteristic of the GEM listing rules (and one of its major attractions for companies considering an IPO) is the entry threshold, which is considerably lower than that of the Main Board.

A main attraction of GEM is that its Listing Rules do not require an applicant company to show a track record of profit.

However, the applicant company must be able to provide information and demonstrate at least two years of an "active business pursuit" immediately prior to the date of the application and show that it is making "substantial progress in building up that business."

---

*Co-authored by Tim Drew, Hong Kong Office, Blank Rome, LLP.

The required period of "active business pursuit" can be lowered to one year for companies that can meet each of the several requirements listed next. (These requirements are not applicable if the company has two or more years of "active business pursuit.")

Financial Record

- The company had a turnover of at least HK$500 million (about $64 million revenue in U.S. dollars based on April 30, 2008, exchange rates) in the past 12 months as reported in the accountants' report; or

- The company had total assets of not less than HK$500 million as of the end of the last financial year shown in the balance sheet as reported in the accountants' report; or

- An expected market capitalization of at least HK$500 million at the time of listing; and

Public Float

- A minimum market capitalization of HK$150 million in public hands; and

Shareholding

- Have at least 300 shareholders, with the largest 5 and 25 holding in aggregate not more than 35% and 50%, respectively, of the equity securities in public hands; and

Offering Price

- An offering price of at least HK$1.

The applicant company must be under substantially the same management and ownership over the relevant period of active business pursuit (i.e., two years or one year). If the active business pursuit is carried on by its subsidiaries, the company must control the boards of those subsidiaries and have an economic interest of not less than 50% in these subsidiaries.

The applicant company must also produce an accountants' report covering the two financial years immediately prior to the date of application, or at least 12 months from commencement of its active business pursuit, if it can satisfy the several requirements just listed. It must also produce a set of business objectives and describe how they are to be achieved.

Companies will have to meet a minimum public float requirement of HK$30 million (approximately $3,840,000 in U.S. dollars based on April 30, 2008, exchange rates) or have at least 25% of the issued share capital in public hands upon listing. For larger companies with a market capitalization of over HK$4 billion, the public float requirement will be the higher of:

- 20% of the total issued share capital; or
- The percentage that would result in the market value of the securities to be held in public hands equalling HK$1 billion

Also, an applicant company must appoint a sponsor (the GEM analog of the Nomad) to assist it with its initial application for listing. A sponsor's role is very important to the successful operation of a GEM-listed company. The sponsor is required to discharge the burden of supervision over the company and to ensure that the company is in compliance with the GEM Listing Rules. GEM also requires a "Compliance Advisor" for a period that begins on the initial listing date and ends on the second fiscal year after the initial listing.

Companies incorporated in Hong Kong, Bermuda, the Cayman Islands, and the People's Republic of China can apply to be listed on GEM. However, companies from other jurisdictions will have to obtain special approval from the Hong Kong Stock Exchange. Note that conglomerates with diversified businesses will not be eligible for listing as they, by definition, do not satisfy the requirement of a focused line of business.

The GEM has a set of governance rules designed to ensure that the market operates fairly, orderly, and efficiently. A GEM-listed company is required to adhere to strict rules and to establish a good business practice. For example, it must:

- Have at least three independent nonexecutive directors on the board, at least one of whom possesses appropriate professional qualifications or related expertise.
- Appoint competent personnel to fill these positions: company secretary, qualified accountant, and authorized representative.
- Establish an audit committee to review the company's financial reports and administer its internal control.
- Designate an executive director as compliance officer.

Some statistics concerning the GEM section of the Hong Kong Stock Exchange as of April 2008 follow.[27]

Number of listed companies	190
Market capitalization (HK$mil)*	118,618
Average price/earnings ratio (times)	17.73

*1 HKD = U.S. $0.128 as of April 30, 2008

SHANGHAI STOCK EXCHANGE

The listing requirements on the Shanghai Stock Exchange are short and sweet and reveal more by what they do not say than by what they do say. An excerpt from these listing requirements follows.

According to the regulations of the "Securities Law of the People's Republic of China" and "Company Law of the People's Republic of China," limited companies applying for the listing of shares must meet the following conditions:

- The shares must have been publicly issued following approval of the State Council Securities Management Department.
- The company's total share capital must not be less than RMB 50 million [approximately U.S. $7.3 million as of July 24, 2008].

- The company must have been in business for more than 3 years and have main profits over the last three consecutive years. In the case of former state-owned enterprises re-established according to the law or founded after implementation of the law and if their issuers are large and medium state-owned enterprises, it can be calculated consecutively. The number of shareholders with holdings of values reaching in excess of RMB 1,000 must not be less than 1,000 persons. Publicly offered shares must be more than 25% of the company's total share capital. For company's [sic] whose total share capital exceeds RMB 400 million, the ratio of publicly offered shares must be more than 15%.

- The company must not have been guilty of any major illegal activities or false accounting records in the last three years.

- Other conditions stipulated by the State Council.

TORONTO STOCK EXCHANGE AND TSX VENTURE EXCHANGE

The Toronto Stock Exchange (TSX) is the largest stock exchange in Canada, and the TXS Venture Exchange is the public venture capital market. Together they are home to the largest number of publicly traded companies in North America, having 9% of all listed companies worldwide. In 2000 the Toronto Stock Exchange became a for-profit company, and in 2001 its acronym was changed to TSX. In 2001 the Toronto Stock Exchange acquired the Canadian Venture Exchange, which was renamed the TSX Venture Exchange in 2002.

There are three tiers on the TSX Venture Exchange. Tier 1 is more senior companies, and Tier 2 companies are considered early-stage or junior companies. Tier 3 is the Canadian version of the U.S. over-the-counter market and is formed primarily of companies from the defunct Canadian Dealers Network.

The listing requirements can be found on the TSX Venture Exchange Web site at www.tsx.com/. Some of the advantages and disadvantages of a listing on the TSX Venture Exchange are cited in

Appendix B of this book. The Canadian version of SOX did not adopt any requirement for an auditor attestation on internal controls, and this may be considered a significant advantage.

The quantitative listing requirements for Tier 2 of the TSX Venture Exchange for technology or industrial companies are extremely liberal, particularly for a Category 3 company, which does not require any revenues or income. A technology or industrial company seeking a listing in Tier 2 must satisfy all the criteria in one of these three categories:

(a) Category 1:

   (i) Net Tangible Assets of at least $500,000;

   (ii) Adequate Financial Resources to carry on the business of the Issuer for 12 months; and

   (iii) Net income of at least $50,000 before extraordinary items and after all charges except income taxes in the fiscal year immediately preceding the filing of the listing application or a minimum average net income of at least $50,000 before extraordinary items and after all charges except income taxes for at least two of the last three fiscal years;

   or

(b) Category 2:

   (i) Net Tangible Assets of at least $750,000;

   (ii) Revenues derived from commercial operations in the last 12 months of at least $250,000;

   (iii) A management plan outlining the development of its business for 24 months, which management plan demonstrates that the Issuer's product, service or technology is sufficiently developed and that there is a reasonable expectation of revenue within the next 24 months; and

   (iv) Adequate Working Capital and Financial Resources to carry out the program outlined in its management plan. For further clarification, adequate Working Capital and Financial

Resources includes the funds necessary to achieve any acquisition, growth or expansion plans and satisfy general and administrative expenses for at least 12 months and at least $100,000
in unallocated funds;

or

(c) Category 3:

   (i) Net Tangible Assets of at least $750,000;

   (ii) At least $250,000 must have been spent on the development
of the product or technology by the applicant Issuer in the
12 months preceding the application;

  (iii) Sufficient testing of any technology to demonstrate commercial
viability;

  (iv) A working prototype of any industrial product;

   (v) A management plan outlining the development of its business
for 24 months, which management plan demonstrates that the
Issuer's product, service or technology is sufficiently developed
and that there is a reasonable expectation revenue within the
next 24 months; and

  (vi) Adequate Working Capital and Financial Resources to carry
out the program outlined in its management plan. For further
clarification, adequate Working Capital includes the funds necessary to achieve any acquisition, growth or expansion plans
and satisfy general and administrative expenses for at least
12 months and at least $100,000 in unallocated funds.

SURVEY

The author surveyed all of the international stock exchanges and requested answers to three questions:

1. What do you view as the primary advantage or advantages of a listing on your stock exchange in connection with an IPO?

2. What do you view as the primary disadvantage or disadvantages of
a listing on your stock exchange in connection with an IPO?

3. Does your stock exchange permit so-called short selling?

Although many international stock exchanges either did not respond or did not give meaningful responses, some exchanges, including the Toronto Stock Exchange, provided thoughtful responses, which are reproduced in Appendix B.

Interestingly, this survey did not reveal any international stock exchanges that prohibited short selling. Short selling is the practice of selling securities that the seller does not then own, in the hope of repurchasing the securities later at a lower price, in an attempt to profit from the expected decline in the price of the security. Short selling, particularly so-called naked short selling (i.e., situations in which the short seller has not identified the stock being sold), has been a problem for many smaller U.S. public companies since it creates a class of investors who are motivated to speak poorly of the company in order to drive down the stock price, which would permit these investors to repurchase the stock at a profit. Naked short selling effectively increases the supply of outstanding stock and drives down its price.

SMALL AND MEDIUM ENTERPRISES MARKETS

Exhibit 9.5 charts the initial public offerings and newly listed companies during 2007 on 30 international small and medium enterprises (SME) markets operated by the various international stock exchanges, including AIM and GEM markets, and the TXS Venture Exchange.[28] These markets are usually dedicated to small and medium businesses, and listing requirements are different from those of the main markets. The OTC markets (e.g., U.S. OTC Bulletin Board and Pink Sheets) and national electronic markets, which are not operated and supervised by a recognized exchange, are not included in the statistics.

In Chapter 10 we discuss the U.S. tax issues in an international IPO for a U.S. private company.

Exhibit 9.5 IPOs and Listings on International SME Markets

Exchange	Market	IPOs	Newly Listed Companies		
			Total	Domestic	Foreign
AMERICAS					
Buenos Aires SE	Pyme Board	0.0	0	0	0
Lima SE	BVL Venture Exchange		5	0	5
São Paulo SE	Organized OTC Market		10	10	0
TXS Group	TSX Venture	500.2	273	273	0
ASIA-PACIFIC					
Bursa Malaysia	Second Board	98.6	8	8	0
Bursa Malaysia	Mesdaq Market	13.9	3	3	0
Hong Kong Exchanges	Growth Enterprise Market	255.6	2	2	0
Jasdaq	NEO	49.9	3	3	0
Korea Exchange	Kosdaq	300.1	68	67	1
New Zealand Exchange	New Zealand Alternative Market	0.2	3	3	0
Osaka SE	Nippon New Market "Hercules"	179.5	28	28	0
Philippine SE	SME Board		0	0	0
Shenzhen SE	SME Board	5,156.0	100	100	0
Singapore Exchange	SGX Catalist	43.7	8	6	2
Thailand SE	Market for Alternative Investment (mai)	90.5	6	6	0
Tokyo SE Group	Mothers	NA	23	22	1

EUROPE—AFRICA—MIDDLE EAST

Athens Exchange	Alex Medium & Small Capitalization Category	15,843.3	1	1	0
Börse Italiana	Mercato Expandi	782.4	11	11	0
Deutsche Börse	Entry Standard	360.0	43	40	3
Euronext	Alternext	620.4	46	42	4
Irish SE	Irish Enterprise Exchange	1,224.8	9	7	2
Istanbul SE	Second National Market	0.0	0	0	0
Istanbul SE	New Economy Market	0.0	0	0	0
JSE	Alternative Exchange	0.0	37	34	3
JSE	Development Capital Market	0.0	1	1	0
JSE	Venture Capital Market	0.0	0	0	0
London SE	AIM	13,198.7	284	197	87
Mauritius SE	Development and Enterprise Market	47.1	7	7	0
OMX Nordic Exchange	First North	1,219.7	55	53	2
Warsaw SE	NewConnect	4.1	24	24	0
Wiener Börse	Second Regulated Market and Third Market	56.4	7	5	2

NOTES

1. Elizabeth Demers (William E. Simon School of Business, University of Rochester) and Phillip Joos (Tilburg University), "IPO Failure Risk" (April 2006), www.simon.rochester.edu/fac/demers/DemersJoosIPOFailures.pdf.

2. Liu Ti, Shanghai Stock Exchange, "Investment Without Risk: An Empirical Investigation of IPO Underpricing in China," Cambridge University (July 2003), http://ssrn.com/abstract=515742.

3. Andreas Oehler (Bamberg University), Marco Rummer (Bamberg University), Peter N. Smith (University of York), "IPO Pricing and the Relative Importance of Investor Sentiment: Evidence from Germany," Department of Economics and Management, Bamberg University, Germany, and Department of Economics and Related Studies, York University, UK (July 2005), http://ssrn.com/abstract=592302.

4. Nitish. Ranjan and TPM. P. Madhusoodanan, "IPO Underpricing, Issue Mechanisms, and Size," Institute for Financial Management and Research, March 22, 2004, http://ssrn.com/abstract=520744.

5. Wan Nordin and Wan-Hussin, "Investor Protection Mechanism and IPO Valuation on the Kuala Lumpur Stock Exchange," School of Accountancy, University Utara, Malaysia (August 2002), http://ssrn.com/abstract=321580.

6. The method of counting record holders is contained in Rule 12g5-1 under the 1934 Act and, in limited circumstances (such as voting trusts known to the company), that rule requires the company to include in the count underlying equity holders.

7. An entity that is a foreign government or any political subdivision of a foreign country is not eligible to be a foreign private issuer.

8. Rule 3b-4 under the Securities Exchange Act of 1934.

9. If the company aggregates the trading of the class of securities in two non-U.S. jurisdictions, the trading for that class in at least one of the two jurisdictions must be larger than the trading for that class in the United States.

10. Rule 12g3-2(b)(iii) provides as follows: "The issuer has published in English, on its Internet Web site or through an electronic information delivery system generally available to the public in its primary trading market, information that, since the first day of its most recently completed fiscal year, it: (A) Has made public or been required to make public pursuant to the laws of the country of its incorporation, organization or domicile; (B) Has filed or been required to file with the principal stock exchange in its primary trading market on which its securities are traded and which has been made public by that exchange; and (C) Has distributed or been required to distribute to its security holders."

    Note 3 to Rule 12g3-2(b)(i) provides in relevant part as follows: "The information required to be published electronically ... is information that is material to an investment decision regarding the subject securities, such as information concerning: (A) Results of operations or financial condition; (B) Changes in business; (C) Acquisitions or dispositions of assets; (D) The issuance, redemption or acquisition of securities; (E) Changes in management or control; (F) The granting of options or the payment of other remuneration to directors or officers; and (G) Transactions with directors, officers or principal security holders ... At a minimum, a foreign private issuer shall electronically publish English translations of the following documents ... if in a foreign language: (A) Its annual report, including or accompanied by annual financial statements; (B) Interim reports that include financial statements; (C) Press releases; and (D) All other communications and documents distributed directly to security holders of each class of securities to which the exemption relates ."

11. Rule 12g3-2 exempts depositary shares evidenced by ADRs (but not the underlying deposited securities) from registration under the 1934 Act if they are registered under the 1933 Act on Form F-6. The registration of the depositary shares under the 1933 Act on Form F-6 does not trigger any reporting requirements under the 1934 Act by reason of Rule 15d-3 of the 1934 Act.

12. Co-authored by Tim Drew, Esq., Hong Kong Office, Blank Rome LLP.

13. For an excellent article on AIM, see Sridhar Arcot, Julia Black, and Geoffrey Owen, "From Local to Global: The Rise of AIM as a Stock Market for Growing Companies," London School of Economics and Political Science (September 2007), www.londonstockexchange.com/NR/rdonlyres/4B0DF62A-BE1E-44F5 -8616-EA2891873F1D/0/AIMshortreport.pdf.

14. www.londonstockexchange.com/en-gb/products/companyservices/ourmarkets/ aim_new/About+AIM/Nominated+Adviser+Search.htm.

15. http://lawprofessors.typepad.com/business_law/2006/08/londons_aim.html.

16. Ibid.

17. www.redherring.com/blogs/pages/print/posts/?bid=57f233e0-2cb3-49df-bgg0 -5714e9.

18. Ibid.

19. Susanne Espenlaub, Arif Khurshed, Abdul Mohamed, "Is AIM a Casino? A Study of the Survival of New Listings on the UK Alternative Investment Market (AIM)," Manchester Business School, 2007, http://efmaefm.org/0EFMSYMPOSIUM/ oxford-2008/Susanne.pdf.

20. Ashley Burrowes, Kevin Jones, "Initial Public Offerings: Evidence from the UK," Emerald Group Publishing Limited, *Managerial Finance,* Vol. 30, No. 1, 2004, pp. 46–62(17).

21. www.londonstockexchange.com/en-gb/about/statistics/factsheets.

22. Sridhar Arcot, Julia Black, and Geoffrey Owen, "From Local to Global: The Rise of AIM as a Stock Market for Growing Companies," London School of Economics (2007) http://www.londonstockexchange.com/NR/rdonlyres/A624F432-5E0E- 4602-8F83-3E1A16E97C62/0/AIMFullreportV5.pdf.

23. Paul Bork, et al.,"World Stock Exchanges: A Practical Guide," Global Business Publishing, Inc. (2007), p. 296.

24. Jean-François Gajewski (professor of Finance at the University of Paris XII) and Carole Gresse (professor of Finance at the University of Paris X—Nanterre and University of Paris IX—Dauphine), "A Survey of the European IPO Market," University of Paris, 2006. Available for purchase: www.ceps.eu.

25. One EUR =U.S. $1.55 as of April 30, 2008

26. Ibid.

27. www.hkgem.com/statistics/ms1/e_MktHighlights.htm.

28. World Federation of Exchanges, Annual Report and Statistics (2007).

U.S. Income Tax Considerations in Establishing or Migrating a Corporation Offshore

Joseph T. Gulant, Esq.
New York Office, Blank Rome, LLP

As discussed in Chapters 1 and 9, there are myriad legal, accounting, and other regulatory benefits of operating a publicly traded corporation outside of the United States. This chapter addresses some of the material income tax issues that arise either when an existing U.S. corporation expatriates to a foreign jurisdiction as a prelude to (or in connection with) an initial public offering (IPO), or where a corporation with U.S. shareholders is a new entity formed in a jurisdiction outside of the United States. As will be discussed, in many cases there are significant tax advantages to be obtained by reestablishing a holding company in a foreign jurisdiction, but there are also some potential tax risks and pitfalls associated with this strategy.

"CORPORATE INVERSIONS": MIGRATION OF AN EXISTING U.S. CORPORATION TO FOREIGN JURISDICTIONS

In the first half of the first decade of the twenty-first century, the U.S. Congress was concerned about a spate of transactions whereby a number of prominent U.S. corporations expatriated to foreign jurisdictions.[1] As the world continues to shrink and the global economy takes hold, Congress was concerned that these corporate expatriations could severely reduce corporate tax revenues in the United States. This concern was based on the notion that although a U.S. corporation is generally subject to income tax on its worldwide income, a foreign corporation is generally subject to income taxation in the United States *solely* on its U.S.-sourced income (e.g., its income attributable to U.S. operations). If successful, a corporation inversion transaction through which a new foreign parent holding company would be established in a low- or no-tax jurisdiction (such as Bermuda or the Cayman Islands) could allow a U.S. multinational corporation to limit its tax exposure in the United States to income derived from its actual operations in the United States and potentially to avoid tax on a large portion of its internationally generated income.

These corporate inversion transactions usually took the form of formations of offshore holding companies with the former U.S. parent corporations becoming subsidiaries of the newly formed foreign parent, or transfers by the U.S. parent corporation of substantially all of its assets to a newly formed foreign corporation. In each case, the shareholders of the U.S. corporation would exchange their stock for stock in the newly formed foreign parent. In response to its concern over the potentially devastating impact that these transactions could have on the U.S. tax base, Congress enacted anti–corporate inversion tax legislation as part of the Jobs Creation Act of 2004.[2]

Under these new rules, if U.S. shareholders (in the aggregate) acquire as part of the corporate inversion at least 80% of the voting power or value or the stock issued by the new foreign parent in exchange for their stock in a U.S. corporation (and, in some cases, interests in U.S. partnerships), then the entity will be treated as a U.S. corporation for U.S. federal income tax purposes (thereby eliminating any potential tax benefits that could otherwise be obtained by the corporate inversion transaction).[3] Alternatively, if the former U.S. shareholders acquire less than 80% but at least 60% of the voting power or value of the stock of the foreign parent, then although the foreign parent will not be treated as a U.S. corporation following the transaction, the former U.S. parent corporation will generally recognize gain in connection with the transaction[4] in an amount equal to the excess of the fair market value of the assets of such U.S. corporation at the time of the transaction over its tax basis (i.e., tax book value) in such assets at that time.[5] This gain recognition represents a sort of tax "toll charge" for the privilege of migrating the U.S. corporation offshore (the 60% gain recognition requirement). Under applicable rules, any such gain generally may not be offset by the U.S. corporation's available tax attributes (such as net operating losses and most tax credits).[6]

Although these corporate inversion rules generally do not apply where U.S. shareholders own (directly or indirectly) less than 60% of the stock of the new foreign parent, certain other rules may apply to cause the former shareholders of the U.S. corporation (and/or the former U.S. corporate parent corporation itself) to recognize taxable gain pursuant to the transaction.

For example, U.S. shareholders of the former U.S. parent will recognize taxable gain, if any, in the United States in connection with an exchange of their stock for stock in the new foreign parent (whether pursuant to a direct stock swap or in connection with an outbound asset transfer by the former U.S. parent to the new foreign parent) if the U.S. shareholders own (in the aggregate) at least 50% or more of the stock of the foreign parent immediately after the transaction.[7] In that case, taxable gain (but not loss) will generally be recognized by the U.S. shareholders (regardless of the size of their percentage interest in the corporation) in an amount equal to the excess, if any, of the fair market value of the foreign parent stock received in the exchange over their tax basis in the stock in the former U.S. parent relinquished in the exchange.[8] In a typical corporate expatriation transaction, the cost of shareholder recognition of gain where the historic U.S. shareholders of the U.S. parent own at least 50% of the foreign parent after the inversion transaction is often viewed by the corporate insiders (i.e., officers and directors) as a reasonable price to be paid for the flexibility and potential future tax benefits involved in the creation of an offshore holding company.

Alternatively, if the U.S. shareholders (in the aggregate) own less than 50% of the new foreign parent corporation after the transaction, then U.S. shareholders who directly or indirectly (through the application of constructive ownership rules) own 5% or more of the voting power or value of the stock of the foreign parent may avoid gain recognition pursuant to the reorganization transaction provided that such 5% shareholders file so-called gain recognition agreements with the Internal Revenue Service. Under these gain recognition agreements, a 5% shareholder generally agrees to recognize taxable gain as of the tax year in which the reorganization transaction took place (plus interest)[9] if certain triggering events occur within the five-year period immediately following the transaction (e.g., a sale by the foreign parent of the stock of the former U.S. parent, a sale by the foreign parent of substantially all of the assets of the former U.S. parent, a sale of the stock of the foreign parent by the U.S. shareholder, etc.). In this case, U.S. shareholders who own less than 5% of the foreign parent corporation following the reorganization transaction generally are not required to file any gain recognition agreements in order to obtain tax deferral in connection with the reorganization (provided that the transaction otherwise qualifies as a tax-free reorganization for U.S. federal income tax purposes).

If structured as either a merger of the U.S. corporation with and into the foreign parent (or with and into a newly formed subsidiary of the foreign parent corporation), or a transfer of the assets of the U.S. corporation to the new foreign parent, then the U.S. corporation will generally recognize gain (but not loss) as if it sold all of its assets for their fair market value as of the date of the transaction (deemed asset sale rule).[10]

In order to avoid this gain, these transactions may be structured as mergers of the U.S. corporation with a newly formed foreign subsidiary of the foreign parent, in a transaction pursuant to which the U.S. corporation (rather than the newly formed foreign subsidiary) survives the transaction. In that event, the transaction is treated as a stock acquisition rather than an asset acquisition, the deemed asset sale rule will not apply, and the transaction may generally be structured to avoid any corporate-level taxes as a result of the transaction (provided that the former U.S. shareholders own less than 60% of the stock of the foreign parent and therefore the 60% gain recognition requirement discussed earlier is not triggered).

PASSIVE FOREIGN INVESTMENT COMPANY AND CONTROLLED FOREIGN CORPORATION ISSUES

The corporate inversion rules just described generally can be avoided if the vehicle chosen for an IPO is a newly formed foreign corporation with no history of operating in the United States. As a general matter and subject to important exceptions, a U.S. shareholder of a foreign corporation is not subject to income tax on such shareholder's share of the income earned by the foreign parent until such income is actually repatriated back to the United States through distributions.

However, U.S. shareholders must be aware of special rules, which will either cause them to be currently taxed on their shares of the income earned by a foreign corporation (regardless of whether such income is actually distributed to them), or, alternatively, cause them to suffer other significant negative tax consequences (such as conversion of income from capital gain into ordinary income taxable at higher tax rates,[11] or the imposition of substantial interest charges on their deferred tax liabilities). A savvy U.S. resident investor must be aware of these potential issues when making an investment in a foreign corporation, regardless of whether a large or small equity position is taken.

As noted, a U.S. shareholder owning a stock interest in a foreign corporation will generally not recognize income from its investment in the foreign corporation for U.S. tax purposes until such time as the foreign corporation pays a dividend to its shareholders. However, as will be discussed, if the foreign corporation constitutes either a passive foreign investment company (PFIC) or a controlled foreign corporation (CFC), U.S. persons who directly or indirectly (through owner-ship in another entity) own shares in the foreign corporation may effectively be subject to tax on the income earned by such foreign cor-poration even if the foreign corporation does not distribute the income to its shareholders in the same year.

PASSIVE FOREIGN INVESTMENT COMPANIES

A foreign corporation will be classified as a PFIC if 75% or more of its gross income for the taxable year is passive income *or* 50% or more of the average value of its assets consists of assets that produce, or are held for the production of, passive income (asset test).[12] For purposes of the PFIC rules, passive income includes div-idends, interest, rents, royalties, annuities, and certain other types of "foreign personal holding company income," as such term is de-fined in the Internal Revenue Code Section 954(c).[13] In determining whether a foreign corporation constitutes a PFIC, if a foreign corpo-ration owns (directly or indirectly) at least 25% (by value) of the stock of another corporation, such foreign corporation will be treated as if: (1) it held its proportionate share of the assets of the other foreign corporation, and (2) it received directly its proportion-ate share of the income of such other corporation.[14] This taxpayer-friendly rule may help foreign holding company parent corporations with subsidiaries engaged in active businesses avoid PFIC status in many cases.

In general, if a U.S. person owns an interest in a foreign corpora-tion that constitutes a PFIC, the U.S. person will either: (1) be subject to an onerous interest charge on the income earned but not distributed by the PFIC at the time that the income is actually distributed to the U.S. person or (2) to the extent that a special election is made by the taxpayer, be subject to income tax in the year that the PFIC earns the income (notwithstanding that the PFIC may not distribute the income to the U.S. person).

Key Distinction. Unlike the rules for CFCs as will be described, these PFIC rules apply *without* any minimum threshold stock ownership requirement. As a result, portfolio investors in a public foreign corporation that constitutes a PFIC will be subject to this oppressive tax regime in the United States *regardless* of their level of stock ownership. In addition, with limited exceptions, once a foreign corporation is treated as a PFIC for any fiscal year, it is treated as a PFIC for all taxable years thereafter, notwithstanding the fact that it may no longer meet the PFIC qualification tests.[15]

In addition, gain on the sale of an interest in a PFIC is generally transmuted from capital gain into ordinary income, and anti–taxpayer rules apply that impose an interest charge on the U.S. shareholder's share of the income earned by the PFIC for all periods (including prior periods) when the entity was a PFIC. For purposes of calculating this interest charge, income earned by the PFIC generally is treated as having been earned on a pro rata basis over the period in which it constituted a PFIC.[16]

CONTROLLED FOREIGN CORPORATIONS

A foreign corporation will constitute a CFC if more than 50% of either the voting power or value of the stock of the foreign corporation is owned (directly or indirectly) by U.S. shareholders.[17] A U.S. shareholder is any person who owns (directly or indirectly) 10% or more of the total combined voting power of all classes of stock entitled to vote of the foreign corporation.[18] For purposes of determining whether a foreign corporation is a CFC, stock in a foreign corporation that is owned through a foreign corporation, foreign partnership, or foreign trust is considered as if owned proportionately by its shareholders, partners, or beneficiaries.[19] There are also "family attribution rules" that constructively treat a U.S. individual as owning, for these purposes, certain stock owned by various family members (including, without limitation, spouses, parents, children, and grandparents).[20] As a result, unless the foreign corporation is effectively "closely held" by U.S. shareholders pursuant to the rules just described, it will not be treated as a CFC.

If the foreign corporation constitutes a CFC, the U.S. shareholders of the CFC will be subject to tax on their respective shares of the CFC's Subpart F income in the year that the CFC earns such income, notwithstanding the fact that the CFC does not distribute the income to the U.S. shareholders.[21] One category of Subpart F income is foreign personal holding company income, which includes dividends, interest, rents, royalties, and annuities.[22] Other income items treated as Subpart F income includes certain related-party sales or service income, certain insurance, and oil-related income.[23]

In addition, gain, if any, on the sale of a U.S. shareholder's ownership interest in a CFC may be transmuted from capital gain into ordinary income to the extent of the U.S. shareholder's share of the undistributed earnings and profits of the CFC (generally retained earnings with certain adjustments), provided that such share of earnings and profits has not been previously treated as Subpart F income that was already taxed in the hands of the U.S. shareholder.[24]

Following an IPO, in light of the U.S. shareholder stockholding requirements attributable to CFCs as described, it is less likely (although possible with respect to closely held foreign public companies) that a publicly traded foreign corporation will constitute a CFC rather than a PFIC. In the event of an overlap, the CFC rules (and not the PFIC rules) apply to any U.S. shareholders (e.g., U.S. persons who own 10% or more of the voting stock of the foreign parent); but the PFIC rules will still apply to any U.S. shareholders who directly or indirectly own less than 10% of the voting stock of the PFIC.

U.S. investors should also be aware of their annual reporting requirements with respect to their ownership of stock in foreign corporations (including ownership interests in CFCs and PFICs).[25] For example, each U.S. shareholder who directly owns at least 10% of the voting power or value of the stock of a foreign corporation or otherwise has controlled a foreign corporation (e.g., a CFC) generally must submit an annual informational statement with his or her U.S. Income Tax Return (IRS Form 5471) describing such shareholder's interest in the foreign corporation and certain specific information relative to the types of income earned by the foreign corporation, a form of balance sheet for the entity and various tax accounting-related information. In these cases, U.S. investors should be aware that cooperation from the foreign corporation will be necessary in order to obtain the information necessary to comply with these rules.

Traditional U.S. IPOs are discussed in Chapter 11. Nontraditional IPOs include reverse mergers into public shells (Chapter 12), mergers into SPACs (Chapter 13), and smaller IPOs, namely Regulation A offerings (Chapter 14) and SCOR offerings (Chapter 15).

NOTES

1. U.S. corporations that either have threatened to or have in fact migrated to foreign jurisdictions include, among others, Stanley Tool Works, Ingersoll-Rand, and Nabors Industries.

2. See the American Jobs Creation Act of 2004 (P.L. 108-357); see generally Section 7874 of the Internal Revenue Code of 1986, as amended.

3. See Code Section 7874(b).

4. Assuming that the U.S. shareholder holds the stock as a capital asset, any such gain will be taxable at long-term capital gains rates for federal income tax purposes (15% for 2008) if the stock has been held for at least one year and a day prior to the transaction, or short-term capital gain (taxable at rates up to 35% for 2008) for federal income tax purposes, if the stock has been held for less than one year and one day at the time of the transaction.

5. See Code Sections 7874(a)(2), 7874(d).

6. See Code Section 7874(e).

7. See Treas. Reg. Section 1.367(a)–3(c)(1).

8. See note 4 for the U.S. federal income tax rates that would likely be imposed on such gain.

9. See Treas. Reg. Section 1.367(a)–8(b).

10. See Code Section 367(a)(5). This automatic gain recognition will not apply, however, if at least 80% of the total combined voting power of all classes of stock entitled to vote and at least 80% of each other class of stock is owned after the transaction by five or fewer U.S. domestic corporations. Ibid.

    Special rules also apply if the U.S. corporation is transferring intangible property (other than goodwill or going-concern value) to a foreign corporation. In that case, the U.S. corporation is generally treated as having sold the intangible property for contingent royalty payments (so-called super-royalty payments taxable as ordinary income rates) over an extended period (generally 20 years), which payments must be commensurate with the income attributable to the intangible property transferred).

11. By way of comparison, the U.S. federal long-term capital gains rate is 15% for 2008, whereas the highest ordinary income tax rate is 35% for 2008.

12. See Code Section 1297(a). The asset test is applied on a gross basis (i.e., no liabilities are taken into account even if the liabilities are directly traceable to an asset). See Notice 88-22, 1998-1 C.B. 489. In computing the average value of a foreign corporation's assets, the corporation must determine the fair market value of its assets on a quarterly basis, as of the end of each quarterly period during the taxable year of such corporation. Ibid. According to Notice 88-22, an asset will be considered passive if it has generated (or is reasonably expected to generate in the reasonably foreseeable future) passive income.

13. See Code Section 1297(b).

14. See Code Section 1297(c).

15. See Code Section 1298(b)(1). The rules provide relief from the application of the PFIC rules for the first year of its operation if, among other items, it would otherwise be treated as a PFIC in its first year but would not be treated as a PFIC in either of the two subsequent tax years. This rule protects many start-up businesses from falling into the web of PFIC status. See Code Section 1291.

16. See generally Code Section 1291.

17. See Code Section 957(a).

18. See Code Section 951(b).

19. See Code Section 958(a)(2).

20. See Code Section 958(b).

21. If this previously taxed income is distributed by the CFC to its U.S. shareholders in a subsequent tax year, it generally passes to the recipient U.S. shareholder without any further imposition of tax in the United States. See generally Code Section 959. It should also be noted that Subpart F income is treated as constructive dividend payments to the U.S. shareholders, which are taxable at ordinary income tax rates.

22. See Code Section 954(c).

23. See generally Code Section 954.

24. See Code Section 1248.

25. See generally IRS Form 5471 (primarily relating to CFCs) and IRS Form 8621 (relating to ownership interests in PFICs).

Part Three

Traditional and Nontraditional IPOs in the United States

Chapter 11

Traditional U.S. IPOs

Traditional U.S. initial public offerings (IPOs) are typically conducted on the New York Stock Exchange (NYSE), The Nasdaq Stock Market (Nasdaq), or the American Stock Exchange.

Once the company has selected an underwriter, preliminary discussions take place concerning the valuation of the company, an underwriter's letter of intent is signed, and the registration process commences. The process ends with a closing at which the shares in the company are issued.

COMPANY VALUATION

Underwriters do not usually value the company until the pricing meeting (the meeting between the company and underwriters' representatives at which the price per share is established), which is held on the effective date of the company's registration statement filed under the Securities Act of 1933 (1933 Act) or a few days thereafter. However, the underwriters should be able to determine the procedure for the valuation at the beginning of the IPO.

Generally, underwriters look at comparable companies that are public and determine their price/earnings multiple or their multiple of

EBITDA (earnings before interest, taxes, depreciation, and amortization). If a comparable company has been public for a while and its market price is 14 times its projected earnings, for example, on the effective date of the IPO registration statement, it may be expected that the company will probably be valued at a 10% to 15% discount below the 14 multiple.

This discount provides an incentive for the institutional investors to buy the company's stock (as opposed to the stock of more seasoned public companies in its industry) on the grounds that the company's stock is a bargain.

If the company is using IPO proceeds to discharge its bank debt or other indebtedness, the underwriter will typically permit the company to increase its earnings or EBITDA by the pro forma interest savings resulting from such discharge of debt.

The company's adjusted earnings or EBITDA are then multiplied by the appropriate multiplier to value the company. For example, if the company's adjusted earnings or EBITDA are $4 million and the discounted multiplier is 12, the company will have a $48 million valuation prior to adjustment for the IPO proceeds. If the company wishes to raise $24 million from the sale of stock in the IPO, its overall valuation will be $72 million ($48 million plus $24 million) and $33\frac{1}{3}$ % of the outstanding stock of the company will be sold in the IPO.

There is a tendency among underwriters to underprice the stock in the initial public offering. Therefore, it may be wise to consider minimizing the total number of shares that the company sells in the IPO. Obviously, the company must balance this consideration against its capital needs at the time the offering goes into effect. A slightly underpriced IPO has the advantage of permitting IPO investors to enjoy a price rise in the aftermarket trading. This may stimulate investor interest in future public offerings by the company. This is particularly important if the company plans a follow-on or secondary offering in the near future.

Underwriters generally tend to price the stock of IPOs between $10 and $20 per share. Occasionally they use an IPO price of $20 or more to create prestige for the issue. If the stock is priced below $5 per share, it is considered a penny stock; brokers trading in penny stocks are subject to onerous Securities and Exchange Commission (SEC) rules that apply to the sales of such securities. The institutional investment community also tends to shun penny stock issues.

To get to a price range of $10 to $20, the company may need to change its stock capitalization (by stock splits or reverse stock splits) to achieve the desired IPO price, based on the valuation of the company and the proportion of the company to be sold in the IPO.

In general, a minimum of 1 million shares are sold in an IPO in order to qualify with the Nasdaq Capital Market publicly held shares requirement, and preferably more than 1 million shares. The purpose of this minimum number is twofold: to make certain there is a sufficient float to permit an active trading market after the IPO and to qualify for the public float requirement to list the stock on the Nasdaq Capital Market. To qualify for the Nasdaq Global Select Market, a minimum of 1,250,000 shares must be sold in the IPO, and a minimum 1,100,000 shares must be sold in the IPO to qualify for the Nasdaq Global Market. Nasdaq does not consider shares held by an officer, director, or 10% shareholder of the company to qualify for these minimums.

LETTER OF INTENT

Once the company has selected an investment banker it is interested in retaining in connection with an IPO, the company will sign a letter of intent. The letter of intent usually is not legally binding (except as will be noted), but it does express the basic business understanding of the parties. The letter of intent typically covers these topics, among others:

- Expected aggregate offering amount (this may be a range)
- Amount of the underwriter's discount (or commissions in the case of a best-efforts offering)
- Any warrants or other consideration given to the underwriter

- Overallotment option, amount of such option, and other terms related thereto
- Who is responsible for the payments of expenses of the underwriters and the offering, such as lawyers, accountants, printers, filing fees, blue sky filing fees, road shows, and other expenses (Is there an underwriter's expense allowance, and is it accountable or nonaccountable?)
- Indemnification rights
- Restrictions on preoffering publication by the company
- Preferential rights on future financings by the company and the period of time these rights are applicable

Unless the company has very strong bargaining power, it is probably wise to agree to give the underwriter, if requested, a preferential right on future financings. However, it is also wise to limit that right to a period not exceeding one year and possibly under the condition that the sale of the company's stock in the IPO be at or close to the price projected by the underwriter.

It is important for the company to designate counsel for the underwriter from a list of counsel approved by the underwriter. Since the company ultimately will pay the fees and costs of the underwriter's counsel, it should have input into this decision as well as negotiate the cap on the amount of the underwriter's counsel's fees and expenses that the company will pay.

Generally a clause is inserted into the letter of intent that requires the company to pay the underwriter's counsel fees and other out-of-pocket expenses in the event the company decides to withdraw from the offering. At a minimum, this clause should be amended to insert a "not to exceed" figure or a "reasonableness" test. In addition, the company may vary the maximum figure by whether the withdrawal occurs early or late in the registration process.

Occasionally, underwriters attempt to insert a clause in the letter of intent providing that if the company is sold before the IPO effective date, and the company withdraws from the IPO, a commission on the sale price should be paid to the underwriter. Such clauses should be carefully reviewed with the company's counsel and, in appropriate cases, rejected.

The letter of intent may also restrict any press releases or other publicity by the company concerning the offering without approval of the underwriter.

The letter of intent does not prevent the underwriter from withdrawing from the IPO. It should be made clear that the company will not reimburse the underwriter for its counsel fees or other expenses if the underwriter withdraws from the IPO without any breach by the company. The best safeguard to the company against the underwriter's arbitrary withdrawal from the IPO is the underwriter's investment of time, counsel fees, and costs in the IPO project as well as the damage to its reputation caused by an arbitrary withdrawal.

TYPES OF UNDERWRITINGS

There are generally two major types of underwritings:

1. Firm commitment
2. Best efforts

In a firm-commitment underwriting, the underwriters agree to buy, at a fixed price, all the securities being sold at a discount from the public offering price. The underwriters then resell the securities to the public at the public offering price. If the underwriters do not resell all the securities, they assume the investment risk with regard to the unsold securities.

Under a best-efforts underwriting, the underwriters agree to use their "best efforts" to sell the securities. However, if the underwriters do not sell the entire amount to the public, they have no obligation to purchase the balance of the shares offered from the company. The underwriters merely act as agent for the issuer of the securities. They are never at risk if the securities are not sold.

There are several variations of the best-efforts underwriting. For example, the agreement may provide that a minimum number of securities must be sold or the purchase price returned to the investors, or alternatively, no minimum is required.

Most IPOs with national or regional underwriters are on a firm-commitment basis. This is the traditional IPO underwriting. Indeed, best-efforts IPOs are relatively rare, and financial markets would view them as a sign of weakness.

As previously noted, even a firm-commitment underwriting is not "firm" prior to executing the underwriting agreement following the pricing that occurs on or shortly after the IPO registration statement's effective date.

COST OF A TRADITIONAL IPO

The largest single cost of the company's IPO is the underwriter's discount from the public offering price. In a firm-commitment underwriting, this normally ranges from 6% to 7% of the public offering price. In a best-efforts offering, the underwriter is paid a commission based on the public offering price, the economic equivalent of the discount. All other factors being equal, the commissions in a best-efforts underwriting should be slightly lower than the underwriter discount since the underwriter assumes less risk.

For example, in the IPO of Orexigen Therapeutics on May 1, 2007, the underwriters' discount was:

	Per Share	Total
Public offering price	$12.00	$84,000,000
Underwriting discount	$.84	$5,880,000
Proceeds, before expenses, to the company	$11.16	$78,120,000

Some underwriters also require the company to pay an expense allowance, which may or may not be on an accountable basis. This is a negotiated figure.

The company will also incur out-of-pocket costs for legal fees and expenses, accounting fees, blue sky fees and expenses, and printing. Legal fees and expenses for the company's own counsel in an IPO are typically between $300,000 and $800,000, but they can substantially exceed $800,000 for particularly complex offerings, such as real estate investment trust offerings. This figure does not include a certain amount of corporate housekeeping that the company may have deferred for a number of years.

Accounting fees and expenses generally run between $300,000 and $500,000. However, they can be much higher if there are significant issues related to the audit.

Printing costs can run between $200,000 and $350,000 or more, depending on the length of the prospectus, the number of copies required, whether the company uses pictures and color, and the extent of the revisions required. Since revisions can be very expensive, it is best not to commence printing until after the company circulates a reasonably good draft to all parties.

Other out-of-pocket costs include SEC filing fees ($55.80 per $1 million for fiscal 2009), blue sky fees and expenses (typically less than $20,000), Nasdaq entry fee ranging from a minimum of $50,000 for the Nasdaq Capital Market to a minimum of $100,000 for the Nasdaq Global Market and Nasdaq Global Select Market, and registrar and transfer fees (generally $15,000 to $50,000).

There are also annual fees charged by the Nasdaq markets ranging from $27,500 per year for the Nasdaq Capital Market to a minimum of $30,000 per year for the Nasdaq Global Market and the Nasdaq Global Select Market.

If the underwriter withdrew very close to the effective date of the offering, it is possible the company could lose anywhere from $300,000 to $700,000 or even higher, even after professional fees have been discounted.

The underwriter is liable for its counsel fees and costs and incurs significant executive time in any underwriting. Therefore, the underwriter has a significant investment that it may lose if it or the company abandons the offering at a late stage.

Exhibit 11.1   IPO Expenses for Orexigen Therapeutics, Inc.

	Amount Paid
SEC registration fee	$ 9,335
NASAD filing fee	9,470
Nasdaq Global Market listing fee	100,000
Legal fees and expenses	800,000
Accounting fees and expenses	450,000
Printing and engraving expenses	250,000
Blue sky, qualification fees and expenses	20,000
Transfer agent and registrar fees	30,000
Miscellaneous expenses	181,195
Total	$ 1,850,000

Exhibit 11.1 is the estimated cost breakdown (excluding underwriters' discount and expense allowance) contained in the $84 million IPO of Orexigen Therapeutics, Inc., on April 2007.

The underwriters' discount totaled $5,880,000. The overall aggregate offering costs of $7,730,000 ($1,850,000 plus $5,880,000) were approximately 9.2% of the $84 million offering (disregarding the 15% overallotment option).

The underwriters' discount in the Drkoop.com, Inc. (June 1999), IPO totaled $5,906,250. The overall aggregate expenses ($1,355,000 plus $5,906,250) were approximately 8.6% of the $84 million offering (disregarding the 15% overallotment option).

DUE DILIGENCE

Under the 1933 Act, the company is absolutely liable if there are material misstatements or omissions contained in the registration statement at the time it becomes effective (unless the purchaser knew of the untruth). In addition, these persons are also liable to investors in such an event, subject to the due diligence defense:

- Directors
- Officers who sign the registration statement (the principal executive and financial and accounting officers)

- Underwriters
- Experts (independent accountants and the like)

The due diligence defense permits these persons (excluding the company) to defend themselves from such liability if they have performed a reasonable investigation and have no reason to believe (and do not believe) that there were any material misstatements or omissions. With regard to the "expertized" portions of the registration statement (such as the audited financial statements), it is sufficient to establish a due diligence defense if these persons have no reason to believe (and do not believe) that there are any material misstatements or omissions.

The underwriters and their counsel spend much time and effort, both prior to filing the registration statement and after filing and prior to its effective date, in an attempt to establish this due diligence defense.

The most famous case on the due diligence defense is *Escott v. Barchris Construction Corporation*. This case arose out of a public offering by a company engaged in the construction of bowling centers, the growth industry of the late 1950s and early 1960s. The investors sued the company and its directors, its officers who signed the registration statement, its auditors, and its underwriters. The court found material misstatements and omissions in both the financial and nonfinancial portions of the prospectuses (e.g., the backlog).

The court held that none of the defendants had established a due diligence defense. The court created different standards of due diligence based on (a) whether a director was or was not an officer and (b) each defendant's background and expertise.

The decision in *Barchris* is also noteworthy in rejecting due diligence defense claims by these directors with respect to the portions of the registration statements other than the audited financial statements:

- Two founding directors and officers—"each men of limited education" for whom the "prospectus was difficult reading, if indeed they read at all"—had no diligence defense. The court stated that "the liability of a director who signs a registration statement does not depend upon whether or not he read it or, if he did, whether or not he understood what he was reading."

- An outside director was liable even though he just became a director on the eve of the IPO and had little opportunity to familiarize himself with the company. The court found that the 1933 Act imposed liability on a director "no matter how new he is." The outside director was not permitted to rely on the statements of other directors and officers of the company who were "comparative strangers" without making further inquiry.

- An outside lawyer director who failed to check on his client's statements to him, which could "readily have been checked," including his client's overstatement of the company's backlog, was held personally liable.

PRESS RELEASES AND PUBLICITY

A discussion of the restrictions under the federal securities laws on publicity during each of these three time periods follows:

- Prior to filing the registration statement (the "gun-jumping" prohibition)
- After filing the registration statement and prior to its effective date
- After the effective date of registration statement and during the continuation of public distribution

PRIOR TO FILING REGISTRATION STATEMENT

Section 5(c) of the 1933 Act generally makes it unlawful to offer to sell any security prior to the filing of a registration statement. This is the "gun-jumping" prohibition. The purpose of this prohibition is to prevent issuers and other persons from arousing public interest in a securities offering prior to the filing of a registration statement.

The term "offer to sell" is broadly defined in Section 2(3) of the 1933 Act to include "every attempt to dispose of a security, for value." Publicity that a company does not express as an offer may nevertheless be construed by the SEC as an offer if it is deemed to involve such an "attempt."

The SEC has taken the position that the release of publicity in advance of a filing that has the effect of conditioning the public mind or arousing public interest in an issuer or in its securities constitutes an offer in violation of Section 5 of the 1933 Act. Upon discovery of such a violation, the SEC will usually delay the effective date of a registration statement in order to allow the effect of such publicity to dissipate.

An exception to this position was created by the adoption of SEC Rule 163A, which provides a safe harbor for communications made by issuers at least 30 days before the filing of a registration statement provided the communication does not reference the public offering and the issuer takes reasonable steps to prevent further distribution or publication of the communication within the 30 days prior to the filing of the registration statement.

The SEC has also taken the position that the prohibition against "offers" of securities prior to filing is not intended to restrict normal communications between issuers and their stockholders or the public with respect to important business or financial developments, provided such communications are consistent with the issuer's prior practice, are in the customary form, and do not include forecasts, projections, predictions, or opinions as to value. Nor does the prohibition affect discussions with underwriters.

In order to determine whether a particular activity or statement by an issuer would constitute an unlawful offer, the facts and circumstances surrounding each activity or statement, including its content, timing, and distribution, must be analyzed. Since this determination often involves difficult legal issues, it is imperative that the company clear any proposed public disclosure with its counsel before its release. Such disclosures would include, but not be limited to, letters to shareholders, product brochures or other marketing materials, press releases, interviews, speeches, advertisements and postings, or content on the company's Web site. The SEC is particularly concerned with publicity that artificially stimulates the markets by whetting the public appetite for the security. The company's Internet Web site must be carefully checked by its counsel.

If the company's offering is a Regulation A offering (discussed in Chapter 14), it can test the waters before filing provided that it complies with certain disclosure requirements, submits the offering material to the SEC, and does not accept any money. However, the company may not raise more than $5 million.

Prior to filing a registration statement with the SEC, the company should conduct a complete review of its Web site, sales and marketing literature, and other public disclosures. Such information should not refer to the company's prospective capital-raising efforts and should be free of exaggerated claims and other false or misleading statements about the company, its products, financial condition, or prospects. In addition, the Web site should not hyperlink to other sites unless those other sites are similarly reviewed.

AFTER FILING REGISTRATION STATEMENT AND PRIOR TO ITS EFFECTIVE DATE

After the filing of a registration statement and before its effective date, the company may make verbal offers to sell securities. Thus, the underwriters may conduct road shows during this period. However, during this period, no written offers may be made except by means of a statutory prospectus (the red-herring prospectus). The underwriters may also place tombstone advertisements during this period. A tombstone ad is an advertisement that provides certain limited information regarding the issuer, its business and the offering, and details about how a prospectus can be obtained.

Any verbal statements made by or on behalf of the company or its proposed underwriters must be consistent with the information contained in the filed registration statement.

The company may not consummate any sales of securities during this period. The prohibition of sales includes a prohibition on contracts of sale as well as the receipt of any portion of the securities' purchase price.

The release of publicity (particularly in written form) during this period also raises a question about whether the publicity is a selling effort by an illegal means, that is, other than by means of a statutory prospectus. Therefore, the company should continue to clear any proposed publicity with its counsel prior to its release.

The SEC rules permit the use of a free writing prospectus by eligible issuers after the filing of a registration statement, provided certain conditions contained in SEC Rules 164 and 433 are met. A free writing prospectus is a written communication that institutes an offer to sell or a solicitation of an offer to buy the securities relating to a registered offering.

AFTER EFFECTIVE DATE OF REGISTRATION STATEMENT AND DURING CONTINUATION OF PUBLIC DISTRIBUTION

After the effective date of the registration statement, the company may make both written as well as verbal offers. However, during the period of the public distribution of the security, a copy of the final statutory prospectus must be delivered in connection with any written offer or confirmation or upon delivery of the security, whichever occurs first. The company may use supplemental sales literature if it accompanies or precedes that literature with a final statutory prospectus. The company may consummate sales during the post–effective date period.

The release of publicity after the effective date and prior to completion of the public distribution likewise raises issues as to whether the publicity is a written offer or supplemental sales literature that must be accompanied or preceded by a final statutory prospectus. Therefore, the company should continue to clear any proposed public disclosure with its counsel until it completes the public distribution.

Prior to the completion of the public distribution, any verbal or written statements must be consistent with the information contained in the prospectus. Although it is not clear exactly when a public distribution has been completed, most lawyers believe that the public distribution period includes, at a minimum, the period after the IPO, during which securities dealers must deliver a prospectus (25 days for securities listed on a national securities exchange) and, if there is an overallotment option, until that option has been exercised or expired.

The period from immediately before the IPO filing until the post-IPO completion of the public distribution of the company's securities is sometimes called the quiet period.

MAJOR IPO PARTICIPANTS AND TIMETABLE

The major participants in the IPO are:

- Company: typically, the CEO and CFO
- Company counsel
- Underwriter
- Underwriter's counsel

Exhibit 11.2 is a typical timetable for an IPO, once a letter of intent with an underwriter has been signed.

Exhibit 11.2   Key Steps in the IPO Process

Stages	Week 1	2	3	4	5	6	7	8	9	10	11	12	13	14
Phase 1 Due diligence	•	•	•											
Draft registration statement	•	•	•	•										
Phase 2 Initial filing with SEC				•										
Preparation of road show and marketing materials					•	•								
Phase 3 Receipt of SEC comments						•	•	•	•					
Printing and distributing of red herrings (preliminary prospectus)								•	•					
Road show presentations									•	•				
Phase 4 Pricing and effectiveness of IPO												•		
Filing of final prospectus with SEC												•		
Closing of IPO														•

The table is misleading, however, because Phase 1 does not begin until a letter of intent is signed, and obtaining an executed letter of intent can take several months to several years. During this period, the company must put its corporate house in order and market the company to potential underwriters. The company should implement the advance planning steps outlined in prior chapters, resolve shareholder issues, and prepare a marketing plan.

Underwriters typically take several months to better understand the company before entering into a letter of intent. Therefore, the company's IPO planning should normally assume that a minimum period of approximately nine months will elapse between the company deciding to go public and actually receiving the funds.

PROSPECTUS

Usually, the company's securities counsel drafts the IPO registration statement and then distributes it to the underwriter, the underwriter's counsel, independent auditors, and executives of the company. The prospectus is Part I of the registration statement. It is the document used to offer the securities to investors. Part II of the registration statement contains other information that, which although filed with the SEC, is not distributed to investors, such as a breakdown of the costs of the offering, indemnification rights of directors and officers, list of exhibits, certain financial statement schedules, and exhibits that include the company's material agreements.

Generally the underwriters and others "wordsmith" the initial draft of the prospectus until it tells a convincing story to potential investors. This process is sometimes laborious and time consuming, and typically occurs at various meetings of all the parties. These all-hands meetings may last through the night.

Of most concern to the underwriters are the prospectus summary, the business description section, the management's discussion and analysis of financial condition and results of operations section, and the use of proceeds section. These sections must present a cohesive and convincing story to investors.

REGISTRATION PROCESS

Once the company files the original IPO registration statement with the SEC, there is generally a quiet period (no marketing or advertising) until the SEC staff issues its comment letter. Typically this occurs approximately 30 days after the filing. Although the SEC staff may decide not to review the IPO registration statement, this is relatively rare.

Once the company receives the comment letter, it prepares revisions to the registration statement, along with supplemental explanations, and files an amendment to the registration statement along with a detailed letter responding to the SEC staff's comment letter. The SEC may require several amendments before it is willing to declare the registration statement effective. All IPO filings with the SEC (as well as most other SEC filings) are required to be made electronically.

In general, the prospectus is not distributed and the road shows are not held until the prospectus has been amended to reflect the SEC's comments.

STATE SECURITIES LAWS

If the company's securities will be authorized for listing on any of these exchanges, it is exempt from state registration requirements:

- New York Stock Exchange (NYSE)
- National Market System of the Nasdaq Stock Market
- American Stock Exchange

Securities listed on these exchanges are also exempt so long as their listing standards continue to be substantially similar to the NYSE and the Nasdaq's National Market System:

- Tier I of the NYSE Arca, Inc. (formerly the Pacific Exchange, Inc.)
- Tier I of the Philadelphia Stock Exchange, Inc.

- The Chicago Board Options Exchange, Inc.
- Options listed on the International Securities Exchange, LLC
- Nasdaq Capital Market (previously known as the Nasdaq Small Cap Market)

The overwhelming number of traditional IPOs meet these requirements. If the company's IPO satisfies these tests, it can skip this section. If the company's securities will be listed or traded elsewhere, such as the OTC Bulletin Board, or the so-called Pink Sheets, this section is applicable to it.

Unless the company is exempt, the registration statement also has to be filed and ultimately approved in the states in which offers and sales will be made. Almost all of the states have securities (blue sky) laws. Some states will not clear IPOs that they consider too speculative or risky. This can occasionally cause serious problems for the marketing of the IPO.

The most common blue sky problem is the prior sale by the company to insiders and promoters of stock at prices substantially below the IPO price (cheap stock). States generally deem prior sales at 85% or less of the IPO price to be "substantially" below the IPO price. The cheap stock issue is typically raised with respect to companies that have no significant earnings or are in the development stage. The usual justifications for cheap stock include:

- The value of the company has increased since the date of issuing the cheap stock.
- The low price for the stock results from resale restrictions.
- Shares were sold to officers and employees at low prices in lieu of normal compensation.
- The number of shares involved is *de minimis*.

If the state securities administrator does not agree with the justification, some states require that the shares be escrowed until the achievement of certain earnings objectives by the company and canceled if those earnings objectives are not satisfied in five or six years.

IPOs, particularly of promotional or developmental-stage companies, can also suffer from some of these blue sky problems:

- Some states may not register the stock if the company's existing capital is less than 10% of the aggregate offering price of the stock sold in the IPO, or if the total cash invested by promoters is less than 10% of the aggregate offering price.

- Some states look with disfavor on excessive numbers of warrants or stock options given to promoters and insiders.

- Some states object to excessive dilution (the difference between the IPO price and the pro forma net tangible book value per share after giving effect to the IPO) if the dilution to new investors exceeds 50%.

- Some states object to insider loans.

- Some states will not register IPOs if the class of stock offered to the public has either no voting rights or less than proportional voting rights. Justifications for the unequal treatment include giving the IPO stock a dividend or liquidation preference.

- Some states object to "blank check" preferred stock (i.e., where the board of directors sets the terms of the preferred stock at some point in the future without shareholder approval).

- Some states object to a company having a negative net worth unless the company projections expect to show profits in a reasonable period of time.

- Some states limit the amount of expenses that the company may incur in a public offering.

Most of these blue sky problems surface in states that have merit review laws. These laws permit a state administrator to determine the substantive merits and fairness to investors of the IPO. This contrasts with the SEC review of IPOs under the 1933 Act, which (theoretically at least) considers only the adequacy of the disclosures made in connection with the offering of securities.

ROAD SHOWS

Sometime after the initial filing date and before the effective date, the underwriter will organize and schedule informational meetings called road shows that showcase the company's executives. These marketing meetings occur at various cities throughout the United States and possibly abroad with potential underwriting syndicate members, portfolio managers, securities analysts, brokers, and institutional investors. The road shows are also coupled with face-to-face meetings with representatives of key institutional investors.

A presentation is usually made by the company (with the underwriter providing assistance), and the audience is given the opportunity to ask questions. The underwriters will rehearse the company on expected questions, and the company's counsel will advise the company officers making the presentation regarding the disclosure guidelines to which the company must adhere.

The road shows (including one-on-one meetings with institutional investors) are usually hectic times for both the underwriter and the company's executives. They involve substantial traveling over a compressed time period, generally ranging from one to two weeks. Company executives should be prepared for a physically grueling schedule. Road shows educate the financial community about the company and generate interest in its IPO.

A few firms broadcast road shows over the Internet, including Bloomberg LP (over its proprietary terminals) and NetRoadshow, a unit of Yahoo! Inc. Almost all of the road shows are prerecorded. However, live road shows over the Internet are emerging as a possible alternative.

PRICING MEETING

The pricing meeting firmly establishes the public offering price for the company's securities. This meeting typically occurs after the close of the market on the day prior to the effective date of the registration statement.

The investment banker will recommend a public offering price based on a number of factors. The most important factor is the price/earnings multiples (or for some companies, the price/revenue multiple) or EBITDA multiples of companies in the same industry that are of comparable size and capitalization and market conditions in general at the time of the pricing meeting. The underwriter also seriously considers the feedback from the road shows. It is important that the company does its own homework in preparing for the meeting. The company should be aware of the price/earnings multiple and EBITDA multiple of comparable companies (including both trailing and projected 12 months), and it should be prepared to negotiate with the underwriters. However, the company's bargaining power is usually very limited. It is generally better to sell the company's stock slightly too cheaply than to have unhappy IPO investors because the aftermarket price falls below the IPO price.

Once the IPO valuation is established, it is common practice to split the outstanding pre-IPO common stock to obtain the correct ratio of new IPO shares to all outstanding shares. For example, assume that the underwriter intends to sell 3 million shares at $15 per share (a total of $45 million) and that the company is valued at $135 million, including the $45 million gross IPO proceeds. The 3 million new IPO shares should equal one-third of all outstanding shares after the IPO, since $45 million gross IPO proceeds equals one-third of the company's $135 million valuation. Therefore, a total 6 million shares should be owned by all pre-IPO shareholders. If the company has only 1 million pre-IPO shares outstanding, it would immediately declare a 6-for-1 stock split. Thus, after the IPO, there would be 9 million shares outstanding; the public would own 3 million shares for the gross proceeds of $45 million, and all pre-IPO shareholders would own 6 million shares.

In the event that a holding company is being formed that will become the parent of the existing private company on the IPO effective date, a similar result can be obtained by adjusting the exchange ratio for exchanging holding company stock for the company's own stock in the existing private company.

EXECUTION OF UNDERWRITING AGREEMENT, LOCK-UP AGREEMENTS, AND EFFECTIVE DATE

The underwriters and the company execute the underwriting agreement on the date (or the evening before the date) it expects the SEC to declare the IPO registration statement effective.

In executing the underwriting agreement, the underwriters legally bind themselves to purchase the company's securities. They must purchase securities at a closing generally held three business days after the date of execution of the underwriting agreement. The underwriting agreement is a complicated agreement and contains a number of outs for the underwriter. The most important outs are:

- A breach by the company of the warranties, representations, or covenants set forth in the underwriting agreement
- The failure to deliver legal opinions, the accountant's "cold comfort" letter (a highly qualified accountant's letter to the underwriter), or other similar documents at the closing
- An order issued by the SEC suspending the effectiveness of the company's registration statement
- The closing of the major trading markets

The underwriting agreement may also contain an overallotment option, also sometimes called a "green shoe." This option typically permits the underwriter to purchase up to a maximum of an additional 15% of the number of shares included in the initial offering. The underwriter can exercise the option only within 30 days of the public offering date. This option permits the underwriter to sell to the public more shares than it must purchase under the underwriting agreement and to cover its short position by exercising the overallotment option.

The company's directors and officers and certain large shareholders will be required to execute a so-called lock-up agreement with the underwriters at or prior to the date of executing the underwriter agreement. A lock-up agreement requires that the signer not sell or otherwise transfer its securities for a period of time, usually six months. However, more than six months may be required for weaker or unusual IPOs. The prohibition on the sale of the company's securities typically also includes a prohibition on short selling, acquiring puts, or other hedging devices.

On the date the SEC declares the company's IPO registration statement effective, it may list the stock on an exchange such as Nasdaq.

The company typically will also register its securities under Section 12 of the Securities Exchange Act of 1934. This registration is required as a condition for listing the company's securities on the national securities exchanges, including Nasdaq. This registration makes the company subject to various periodic reporting requirements, proxy rules, tender offer rules, short-swing profit rules, and the like.

DIRECTED SHARES

Most underwriters will permit 5% to 10% of the total number of shares to be sold in the IPO to be directed to family and friends. Care should be taken in directing shares to customers or their purchasing agents, since this could result in public disclosure and possible embarrassment. Some underwriters are considering making the company liable if some of these directed shares are not paid for by its family and friends and cannot otherwise be easily sold.

CLOSING

The closing is generally held three business days after the execution of the underwriting agreement. At the closing, the company and other selling shareholders receive payment (typically in next-day funds) and the underwriter receives the company's securities.

NONTRADITIONAL IPOS

The next four chapters discuss nontraditional IPOs. These include the following. Chapter 12 discusses reverse mergers into public shells; Chapter 13 covers reverse mergers into special-purpose acquisition companies (SPACs); Chapter 14 deals with Regulation A offerings; and Chapter 15 covers SCOR (small corporate offering registration) offerings.

A reverse merger of a private company into a public shell or into an SPAC (or an SPAC subsidiary) creates a public trading market for the former shareholders of the private company. A reverse merger into a public shell that has no capital is not really the equivalent of an IPO unless capital is raised in connection with the reverse merger, in contrast with a reverse merger into an SPAC (or SPAC subsidiary), which is required by SEC rules to have at least $5 million in capital. Unless the board of directors of the public shell or SPAC is controlled after the reverse merger by the former shareholders of a private company, the transaction is more analogous to a sale rather than an IPO. Accordingly, if the intent of the reverse merger is to effectuate an IPO, the former private company shareholders must control the board of directors of the public company after the reverse merger.

A Regulation A offering permits a private company to raise up to $5 million in capital during a 12-month period and is a method for smaller private companies to go public. An SCOR offering permits a private company to raise up to $1 million in capital during a 12-month period and is also a method for a smaller private company to go public. Since both Regulation A offerings and SCOR offerings are exempt from the registration provisions of the 1933 Act, each has the advantage of not subjecting the company to the requirements of SOX.

Other nontraditional IPOs include intrastate offerings registered in one state where the securities are offered and sold only to residents of that state and offerings outside of the United States typically pursuant to SEC Regulation S. Neither of these types is discussed in this book.

Chapter 12

Reverse Mergers into Public Shells

Jane K. Storero, Esq.

Philadelphia Office, Blank Rome, LLP

Although the traditional method of going public in the United States involves the sale of stock through an underwriter followed by the commencement of trading of such stock on an exchange, the reverse merger offers an alternative means of going public.[1] In Chapter 13 we discuss reverse mergers into a *special-purpose acquisition company* (SPAC). However, there are many other types of reverse mergers, including mergers with a public shell other than an SPAC.

The Securities and Exchange Commission (SEC) defines a *shell company* as a company that has filed a registration statement under the Securities Act of 1933 (1993 Act) (subject to a limited exception for asset-backed issuers) that has either no or nominal operations and:

- No or nominal assets *or*
- Assets consisting solely of cash and cash equivalents *or*
- Assets consisting of any amount of cash and cash equivalents and nominal other assets[2]

For purposes of this chapter, a *public shell* is any company that has a significant number of public shareholders and little or no operations, whether it technically satisfies the SEC definition of a shell company or a Rule 419 blank-check company (discussed later in this chapter). The public shell may have no operating business whatsoever or may have only a minor business that it operates, or it may have a major business that it previously operated whose assets were sold to a third party. A public shell can also include public companies that previously filed for bankruptcy, disposed of their assets for the benefit of creditors, and have received a bankruptcy discharge. Some public shells are "manufactured" by promoters who wish to profit from the merger of the private company into the public shell. These off-the-shelf shells are *clean shells,* as they have no prior operating history, but often have a more limited shareholder base than the traditional legacy shells.

It has been reported that these well-known companies have gone public through reverse mergers:[3]

- Berkshire Hathaway, Inc.
- Blockbuster Entertainment
- Muriel Siebert & Co., Inc.
- The New York Stock Exchange
- Occidental Petroleum Corporation
- Tandy Corporation (Radio Shack Corporation)
- Texas Instruments, Inc.

A merger with a public shell provides the means of achieving a company's objective of "being public" and accessing the public capital markets without the expense and time involved in doing a traditional initial public offering (IPO). A merger with a public shell is often utilized by companies that are too small to attract the interest of an underwriter or when the market for a traditional IPO does not exist. A merger with a public shell is often selected by a company that is unable to wait the six-plus months necessary for the completion of the traditional SEC registration process.

A merger with a public shell involves the merger of the private company with a public shell through a reverse direct merger (i.e., the private company is merged into the public shell) or, more commonly, through a reverse triangular merger into a subsidiary of the public shell. This transaction is referred to as a reverse merger transaction because the private company merges with the public shell, or a subsidiary of the public shell, and, following the merger, control of the public shell rests with the former stockholders of the private company.

The merger of a private company with the public shell does not, in itself, provide the private company with any capital. This contrasts sharply with a merger into an SPAC, discussed in Chapter 13, which by definition has at least $5 million in capital and, typically, substantially more. Some public shells that are not SPACs do have a small amount of capital, but most do not. Accordingly, unless the public shell merger contemplates raising new capital, preferably in a private equity transaction with registration rights (also called a PIPE—private investment public equity—transaction) simultaneously with the merger, or has sufficient cash to fund its operations and expansion plans, a merger with a public shell has all of the disadvantages of an IPO (including significant dilution from the public shareholders of the shell) and very few of the advantages.

The major advantage of a reverse merger into a public shell with no capital is the potential to raise capital in the future because of the public trading market and, to a lesser extent, the ability to use stock of the public shell after the merger to make further acquisitions. To obtain this advantage, it is important that the public shell have a public trading market and ticker symbol, preferably prior to the merger.

MECHANICS OF REVERSE MERGERS

To become part of a public shell, the private company (also called the "operating company") typically merges into a public shell or with a subsidiary of the public shell in a triangular merger, which is discussed below. Prior to the merger, the private company and the shell's promoter negotiate a percentage of the shell's stock that the private company's shareholders would receive in the merger in exchange for the stock of the operating company. The percentage of stock the shell's stockholders receive depends on whether the shell has capital and the relative valuation of the private company as compared to the shell company. If the public shell has no capital, the shell company stock the private company receives in the reverse merger would typically equal 80% to 95% of the total outstanding stock.

In the Muriel Siebert Capital Markets, Inc./J. Michaels, Inc. merger (November 11, 1996), Muriel Siebert, the sole shareholder of the private company, received 97.5% of J. Michaels, Inc. stock, and the public shareholders of J. Michaels, Inc. received the remaining 2.5%. At the other end of the spectrum, in May 2008, KY USA Energy, Inc. merged with a subsidiary of a public shell (previously known as Las Roca Mining Corp., whose name was changed to Kentucky USA Energy, Inc.), and its shareholders wound up with slightly more than 50% of the shares of the public shell.

More recent reverse mergers involve the share exchange on October 9, 2007, of OmniaLuo, Inc. (OTCBB: OLOU) with Wentworth II, Inc., a public shell company. OmniaLuo, based in China's fashion capital of Shenzhen, is engaged in the business of designing, developing, marketing, and distributing fine women's apparel under the name OMNIALUO. Contemporaneously with the share exchange, OmniaLuo completed a private placement of common stock and warrants that produced gross proceeds of approximately $6 million.

Similarly, on December 21, 2007, Bonds.com Group, Inc. (OTCBB: BDCG) completed a reverse merger with IPORUSSIA, Inc. and raised gross proceeds of approximately $4 million in a private placement.

In the triangular merger transaction (see Exhibit 12.1), the public shell company creates a merger subsidiary that is owned 100% by the public shell company. The merger subsidiary then merges with the private company, with the private company typically surviving the merger. Shares of the private company are, as a result of the merger, exchanged for a sufficient number of shares of the public shell company to constitute control. After the merger, the private company becomes a wholly owned subsidiary of the public shell company, and the shareholders of the private company now control at least a majority of the stock of the public shell company.

If the public shell is subject to the proxy rules under the Securities Exchange Act of 1934, the public shell must file a merger proxy statement with the SEC that contains audited financial statements from both the private company and the public shell, including pro forma combined financial information, and wait for comments from the SEC.

ADVANTAGES OF A REVERSE MERGER

The advantages of utilizing a reverse merger to go public versus a traditional IPO are:

- **Expeditious process.** Typically, a reverse merger can be completed much faster than a traditional IPO. A typical IPO can take six to nine months or longer to complete; a reverse merger can be completed in approximately three months if financing is included in the process or two months if no financing is involved. The reason for this significant time differential as compared to a traditional IPO is that the underwriter's due diligence process and the SEC staff review take a considerable amount of time to complete. A reverse merger typically involves only a few controlling shareholders of the public shell and a limited number of shareholders of the private company and their attorneys and other advisors.

- **Reduced costs.** A traditional IPO not only takes longer but is significantly more costly than a reverse merger. Legal, accounting, and underwriting fees are significantly higher with a traditional IPO than with a reverse merger due to the liability of the parties as well as the time and cost associated with the preparation of a prospectus and registration statement, which are subject to SEC review. In a traditional IPO, the company does not have the

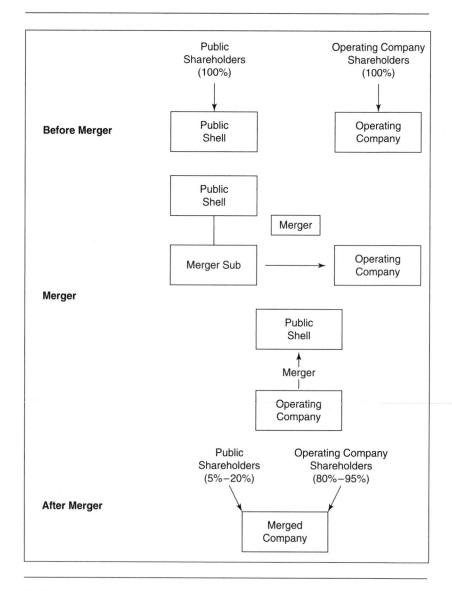

Exhibit 12.1   Shell Mergers

assurance of knowing how much capital it will actually receive until the effective date of the IPO, after it has already spent substantial sums. In a public shell transaction, the most significant costs

are the cost of the public shell itself and the investment banking fees associated with the financing that is frequently undertaken. Costs associated with public shells vary depending on whether it is a trading shell (i.e., the shell's stock trades on the Pink Sheets) or a reporting shell (i.e., the shell's stock trades on the OTC Bulletin Board), the supply and demand for shells at the time of the transaction, how clean the shell is, and the breadth of the shell's shareholder base, as well as the amount of cash and other assets held by the shell.

- **Market factors and underwriters irrelevant.** Unlike traditional IPOs, reverse mergers are not contingent upon market conditions. Frequently, in an unstable market such as that experienced after the Internet implosion and market crash in April 2000 or the corporate scandals that sent shocks through the market after the Enron and WorldCom bankruptcies in 2002, underwriters were reluctant to take public anything but large well-established companies. Reverse mergers, however, do not involve the sale of shares into a public trading market and do not require the assistance of an underwriter. As a result, reverse merger transactions are not typically impacted when market conditions for traditional IPOs are weak. SPACs, which are a form of public shell described in Chapter 13, can also be utilized in a weak IPO market due to the unique characteristics and investor protections available to SPAC investors that do not exist in traditional IPOs or in reverse mergers.) In addition, in a reverse merger, there is no risk that the underwriter will withdraw or determine not to go forward, as typically an underwriter is not involved in a reverse merger transaction. If a financing is necessary in connection with a reverse merger, that financing typically is undertaken as a private placement prior to or simultaneously with the consummation of the reverse merger transaction.

- **Possible immediate trading market.** After the merger, the existence of a public trading market in the company's stock is very useful in attracting additional capital, since the market provides immediate liquidity for the investor.

- **Reduced dilution.** In a reverse merger, the financing, if any, that is undertaken tends to be smaller than in a typical IPO. As a result, the dilution to existing investors is typically less in a reverse merger, which allows the private company shareholders to retain a greater percentage ownership in the resulting company. In a reverse merger transaction, the existing shareholders of a public shell retain some ownership in the resulting company; however, their percentage ownership tends to be negotiated and is typically insignificant. The percentage ownership of shell company stockholders is typically based on the amount of cash or other assets held by the public shell prior to the merger and the need to maintain a meaningful public float.

- **Existence of tax loss carryovers.** If the shell has a tax-loss carryover, that carryover, subject to significant limitations, may be available to shelter the taxable income of the company's business.

DISADVANTAGES OF A REVERSE MERGER

There are also major disadvantages of the reverse merger with a public shell.

- **Lack of capital.** If the shell has no capital, the company still has no assurance until after the merger as to how much capital it can raise and what valuation the market will give to the company.

- **Shell promoters.** Some shells are promoted by less than the best quality broker-dealers, who typically maintain large spreads between the bid and ask prices for the company's stock (enlarging their profits or commissions). Care should be taken in investigating the background of promoters of shell and other blank-check companies. Some of these promoters have questionable backgrounds and should be avoided.

- **Shell stigma.** There is a certain stigma to shell mergers, which may prevent financing by some of the traditional capital sources;

however, the company may not have qualified for financing by such traditional sources even if no shell merger ever occurred.

- **SEC rules.** The SEC disfavors shells due to abuses resulting from the activities of management of some shells, which resulted in disclosure abuses and securities law violations. As a result, the SEC has adopted more stringent rules applicable to shell companies and has limited the ability of shell companies to utilize certain short-form registration statements.

- **Valuation/liquidity.** A private company that undertakes an IPO begins trading on a national securities exchange immediately and has an investment banker that is supporting its stock and has added credence to its valuation. Most shell merger companies do not have this advantage. Additionally, the post-combination company will continue to trade on the Pink Sheets or the OTC Bulletin Board even if it meets the listing requirements of a national securities exchange until it is approved for listing, which can take several months. For these reasons, the post-combination company's stock is likely to be illiquid and will not have an institutional following. As a result, the market price of the stock may not reflect its true value.

- **Undisclosed liabilities.** As a final consideration, the shell may have undisclosed liabilities that the private company business will inherit. This can result in significant issues if the shell is not clean.

OTHER CONSIDERATIONS

The promoters of the public shell typically have a relationship with broker-dealers who make a market in the shell stock after the merger and assist in raising additional capital. The promoters of the shell typically receive warrants and stock in the merged company. The promoter's stock ownership is included in the public stock ownership after the merger shown in Exhibit 12.1. If the shell has cash or other assets, the ownership by the public and promoters after the merger increases proportionately.

After the merger, the company should not suffer the same liquidity discount that applies to a privately held company. Numerex Corp., which was traded on the Nasdaq Stock Market, is an example of a company that went public through a shell merger and then raised over $40 million in a traditional Public Offering.

The depth of the public market after the shell merger is crucial to the success of any further capital-raising efforts. If only one broker-dealer is making a market in the stock after the shell merger, investors will be rightfully leery of the market's liquidity. The company should carefully investigate the background of the promoters of public shells prior to engaging in any shell merger. An ounce of prevention is worth a pound of cure.

As noted, the coupling of a private placement of securities (typically under Rule 506 (promulgated under the 1933 Act) with a shell merger is a useful device. The private placement permits the company to raise capital simultaneously with the shell merger. The shell merger creates a public trading market for the private placement securities, subject to subsequent registration or an exemption therefrom. As a result, the investors typically can justify a higher valuation for the company since there is no need for a liquidity discount.

ALTERNATIVE TO REVERSE MERGER

A statutory merger of a private company into a public shell or the subsidiary of a public shell is not the only method of going public. A faster method of combining with a public shell is to have the shareholders of the private company transfer their shares to the public company in a tax-free exchange for at least 80% of the total combined voting power of all classes of stock entitled to vote and at least 80% of the total number of shares of all other classes of stock of the public shell corporation. The transaction must qualify under Section 368(A)(1)(B) of the Internal Revenue Code to be tax free.

The public shell must have sufficient authorized but unissued shares of common stock so that the shareholders of the private company can satisfy the 80% requirement after the exchange. The exchange would be conditioned on the resignation of the directors and officers of the public shell and their replacement by directors and officers of the private company. If the public shell is subject to the proxy rules of the 1934 Act, the public shell would have to make full disclosure of the change in directors to the SEC and all holders of record of its voting securities pursuant to Section 14(f) of the 1934 Act at least 10 days prior to the new directors taking office. This transaction structure will work only if the public shell has a private placement or other exemption from the registration provisions of the 1933 Act with respect to the shares of the public shell issued to the shareholders of the private company.

The major advantage of this new structure is that there is no need for the public shell to file a merger proxy statement with the SEC and to wait for comments and changes from the SEC staff.

SEC REGULATION OF BLANK-CHECK COMPANIES: RULE 419

SEC Rule 419 governs registration statements filed under the 1933 Act relating to offerings by so-called blank-check companies. Care must be taken in merging with public shells to determine whether they may be considered blank-check companies under Rule 419 and, if so, to determine whether they have complied with Rule 419, since unscrupulous promoters seek to evade that rule.

Under Rule 419, a *blank-check company,* which is similar but not identical to a shell company, means a company that satisfies both of these criteria:

- It is a development-stage company that has no specific business plan or purpose or has indicated that its business plan is to engage in a merger or acquisition with an unidentified company or companies, or other entity or persons.
- It is issuing "penny stock," as defined in SEC Rule 3a51-1 under the 1934 Act.

A *penny stock,* excludes, among other securities, any equity security whose issuer has:

- Net tangible assets (i.e., total assets less intangible assets and liabilities) in excess of $2 million, if the issuer has been in continuous operation for at least three years, or $5 million, if the issuer has been in continuous operation for less than three years; *or*
- Average revenue of at least $6 million for the last three years.

Rule 419 was adopted by the SEC to address the abuses that arose when shell companies engaged in a public offering and then intended to do a merger with an identified private company at a later date. Rule 419 requires that in such circumstances, the gross proceeds of the offering be deposited in an escrow account less certain permitted deductions. Rule 419 limits offering expenses to 10% of the offering proceeds in addition to customary underwriting commissions. Under Rule 419, the stock issued in the offering must be placed into escrow until the merger with the private company is consummated. In order to achieve the release from escrow of the stock and proceeds, three conditions must be met:

1. The business acquired must have a fair market value equal to at least 80% of the maximum offering amount.
2. Investors must reconfirm their investment decision after receiving information regarding the company to be acquired.
3. The merger must be completed within 18 months of the public offering.

An SPAC is exempt from Rule 419 because, after its IPO, it has $5 million or more of net assets, provided it file a Form 8-K indicating such after its IPOs is consummated.

In July 2005, the SEC adopted new requirements applicable to shell companies, which could include blank-check companies.[4] The new shell company rules require the filing of a current report on a

Form 8-K within four business days of the closing of a reverse merger transaction if the transaction results in a change of control or change of the shell company into a non-shell company. The Form 8-K must include the information that typically would be included in a registration statement on Form 10 regarding the private company merged with the public shell. A Form 10 is the registration statement used by a company to voluntarily register a class of its securities with the SEC under the 1934 Act. This information is similar to that which would be included in a prospectus for a traditional IPO and includes:

- At least two years of audited financial statements (or three years if the company does not qualify as a small business)
- A description of the private company's business
- Risk factors related to the business
- A description of related-party transactions
- Executive compensation disclosure
- A description of the private company's capital stock
- A description of all private offerings of securities completed by the private company in the last two years
- Five years of biographical information on the directors and certain executive officers of the private company
- Ownership information of the directors, executive officers, and 5% shareholders of the private company
- Management's discussion and analysis of financial condition and results of operations
- A discussion of the private company's liquidity and capital resources.

In addition, material contracts and other documents, such as the private company's articles or certificate of incorporation and bylaws, must be filed as exhibits to the Form 8-K.

The rules also provide that a shell company may not use a registration statement on Form S-8 to register shares for issuance to the company's employees or consultants. A Form S-8 is a short form registration statement that typically is used to register shares issued pursuant to benefit plans to directors, officers, employees, or consultants who are natural persons of a public company. The advantage of a Form S-8 is that it is automatically effective upon filing with the SEC and the company utilizing this form does not have to undergo a lengthy review process by the SEC staff. Since this short form registration is not available to shell companies, a shell company must wait at least 60 days after its change in status to utilize this form.

The shell company rules also include a box on the front cover of quarterly and annual reports filed by reporting companies with the SEC that requires such companies to indicate whether the filing company is a shell company as defined under the SEC definition as given earlier in the chapter.

NOTES

1. See generally W. Sjostrom Jr., "The Truth about Reverse Mergers," *Entrepreneur Business Law Journal* 2, No. 2 (2008): 231 et seq.

2. Rule 12b-2 under the 1934 Act.

3. D. Feldman and S. Dresner, "Reverse Mergers: Taking a Company Public without an IPO," Bloomberg, 2006.

4. SEC Rel. No. 33-8587. This reason only applies if the shell company is required to file reports under section 13 or 15(d) of the 1934 Act.

Chapter 13

Using a SPAC to Go Public

Brad L. Shiffman, Esq.
New York Office, Blank Rome, LLP

INTRODUCTION

A relatively new entrant into the merger and acquisition market is the special-purpose acquisition company (SPAC), an entity whose assets consist entirely of cash and cash equivalents. A SPAC is a publicly traded "blank-check" company, formed for the purpose of effecting a business combination with an unidentified operating business. A merger of a private operating company into a SPAC or a subsidiary of a SPAC is a method for the private company to go public.

There are two types of blank-check companies:

1. Blank-check companies that are subject to Securities and Exchange Commission (SEC) Rule 419, discussed in Chapter 12.
2. Structured blank-check companies, such as SPACs, which are exempted from SEC Rule 419 because they have net tangible assets of $5 million or more or are otherwise exempt from SEC Rule 419

SPACs have substantially more than the $5 million necessary to exempt themselves from SEC Rule 419. The average size of a SPAC initial public offering (IPO) in 2007 was $183 million.

SPACs have much to offer as a potential business combination partner. In fact, a SPAC can be viewed as an ultimate reverse merger partner. This is because a SPAC has all of the characteristics of a shell company: It is publicly traded and has a sizable public float. A SPAC has several advantages over an ordinary shell company, though. A SPAC is exceedingly "clean." A SPAC has never had an operating business, and its history is easy to track, as its formation date and the date of its initial public offering are easy to ascertain through its public filings on the SEC's EDGAR database. Therefore, unlike many combined companies, a SPAC has no skeletons in its closet. Most important, unlike a typical shell, a SPAC has plenty of cash that can be used to pay a portion of the acquisition consideration, used to fund the post-combination company's working capital, or set aside as a war chest to fund future acquisitions. Additionally, many SPACs are exchange listed, often on the American Stock Exchange, which makes listing on an exchange simultaneously with the business combination more likely than in a traditional reverse merger since the exchange's review is often simpler.

SPACs also offer advantages over private equity funds for target companies because of their cash position and the liquidity they offer. Although it is true that the owners of a target company will be required to accept a portion (often a substantial portion) of their consideration in capital stock for a "business combination" to be approved by the SPAC's stockholders (for reasons to be explained in this chapter), the SPAC's cash makes it an attractive candidate because the owners can partially cash out and have a stronger company post-combination with the infusion of the SPAC's remaining cash. Because of its strong cash position, a SPAC also does not need to take on as much debt as most private equity firms do to complete an acquisition.

A SPAC also offers an attractive alternative compared to a business combination with a strategic partner. A SPAC's advantages include:

- The liquidity of its publicly traded stock following the business combination

- The cash the combined entity will retain
- The fact that the target company's owners (as a group) often control the combined company

An additional benefit is the probable higher value of the company after the transaction, as public companies often trade at higher multiples than private companies. In addition, members of the target company's management are also more likely to keep their management roles following a merger with a SPAC than they would be if the company was acquired by a competitor, as a competitor would likely seek to consolidate the target's management with its own personnel.

In light of the subprime crisis that began in 2007 and the resulting credit crunch in which many firms find it hard to finance their debts, a SPAC's cash position makes it an even more compelling alternative for private companies.

A SPAC is a highly motivated buyer that has a significant advantage over many other buyers because of its ability to use its cash and publicly traded stock to finance an acquisition. Members of a SPAC's management team are also highly motivated, since their equity in the SPAC will be lost if they do not complete a business combination, and they have only a limited time to complete a transaction after their IPO. Once a SPAC identifies a target opportunity it would like to pursue, it can move quickly through the transaction process from a letter of intent, to due diligence, to a definitive agreement.

A seller considering a SPAC as a potential suitor must realize that there are disadvantages in attempting to complete a business combination with a SPAC. The disadvantages of a business combination with a SPAC derive from the unique stockholder protections built into the SPAC structure (which are explained later in this chapter under the caption "SPAC Features Relating to a Business Combination"). The SPAC's public stockholders must approve the SPAC's initial business combination. The SPAC is required to solicit stockholder approval through a proxy statement, and, unless the SPAC is a foreign private issuer, the proxy statement must be filed with and reviewed by the SEC. Because the proxy statement will be the first public filing with information about the target company, it will likely be highly scrutinized by the SEC. As a result, the timing of a transaction from signing a letter of intent to the completion of the transaction is unpredictable and often lasts more than six months. Additionally, because the SPAC's stockholders must approve the transaction, consummation of the transaction is far from certain.

WHAT IS A SPAC?

OVERVIEW

Similar to a private equity fund, a SPAC typically is managed by an experienced management team and group of advisors. SPAC management teams generally have experience completing acquisitions, investing in private equity, and/or managing companies or expertise within a specific industry (from which the SPAC will seek its business combination target). Essentially, a management team raises funds through an initial public offering and then seeks out a transaction with a viable operating company.

The first SPAC was completed in the mid-1990s, but the demand for SPACs disappeared quickly because of the strong IPO market. The SPAC market reemerged in 2003 and has become more than just a niche market in the past couple of years. As of April 1, 2008, 156 SPACs had completed their IPOs. Of that number, 49 had consummated a business combination, 23 more announced agreements relating to a potential transaction, and 12 announced they were liquidating for failure to complete a transaction. Many SPACs are listed on the American Stock Exchange, and, in early 2008, both the New York Stock Exchange and the Nasdaq Stock Market have announced new rules to permit the listing of SPACs, subject to SEC approval.[1] Top-tier investment banks, such as Citigroup, Deutsche Bank and UBS Securities, are underwriting SPACs. High-profile offerings, including Nelson Pelz's Trian Acquisition Corp., which raised $920 million, and Tom Hicks's Hicks Acquisition Company I, Inc., which raised $552 million, have brought legitimacy and a lot of interest to this market.

Not only has the number of SPAC IPOs increased over the past several years, SPACs were larger in 2007. During 2007, the 66 SPAC IPOs represented approximately 22% of all IPOs, compared to 37 SPAC IPOs, or approximately 16% of all IPOs, during 2006. The average size of the SPAC IPOs in 2007 was over $183 million, compared to approximately $90 million in 2006, $74 million in 2005, and under $40 million in 2004. In December 2007, Liberty Acquisition Holdings Corp. completed the first $1 billion SPAC IPO. As of September 1, 2008, the 58 SPACs seeking to complete acquisitions had approximately $12 billion in trust.

Chief among the characteristics that distinguish a SPAC from a traditional blind pool are its public stockholder protections. The most important of these protections are the rights given to such stockholders (a) to vote on each business combination proposed for the SPAC, until one has been approved by the public stockholders and consummated, and (b) to elect, at the time they place their vote, if they are voting against the proposed transaction, to have their stock converted into their proportionate share of the proceeds held in the SPAC's trust account (to be described under "SPAC Features Relating to a Business Combination" later in this chapter) concurrently with the closing of the transaction.

ECONOMICS

Before considering a business combination with a SPAC, the principals of a private company must understand the economics of a SPAC.

In typical SPAC IPOs, the SPAC sells units to the public, consisting of one share of common stock and one common stock warrant. The share and warrant will become separately traded in most offerings within 90 days of the IPO. Each warrant entitles the holder to purchase one share of stock at a price that has been set at a discount to the price of the public unit. The warrant typically becomes exercisable upon the later of (a) the SPAC's completion of its initial business combination and (b) the first anniversary of its IPO.

Prior to the IPO, in most cases when the SPAC's corporate entity is first formed, the SPAC's insiders (its officers, directors, and advisors and their affiliates) generally purchase, for a nominal sum (typically $25,000), such number of shares of stock as will equal 20% of the SPAC's total outstanding shares immediately following the IPO. For example, if the SPAC plans on selling 10 million shares of its stock in the IPO at an offering price of $10.00 per share (a $100 million IPO), the insiders will purchase 2.5 million shares, representing 20% of the 12.5 million shares that will be outstanding after the IPO, for $25,000. As a result, upon completion of the IPO, they will own $25 million worth of stock, based on the IPO price.

Substantially all of the proceeds of the SPAC's IPO are placed in a trust account for the benefit of the public stockholders. Historically, 85% to 90% of the gross proceeds were placed in the trust account, and no withdrawals from the account were permitted prior to the SPAC's initial business combination. Currently, however, in response to market demand, SPACs are placing 99% to 100% of the gross proceeds from their IPOs in the trust account (such that, often, only $50,000 to $100,000 of the IPO proceeds are being retained by the SPAC outside of the trust). SPACs have been able to accomplish this and still have sufficient monies to pay their IPO expenses and fund their pre-combination operations as a result of three measures:

1. A portion of the interest earned on the trust account may now be withdrawn from the account to pay some of the SPAC's working capital expenses and taxes prior to its initial business combination.

2. The SPAC's insiders are now, in addition to their share purchases previously discussed, making more substantial investments in the SPAC at the time of the IPO, through a simultaneous purchase of warrants or units (typically for a purchase price equal to 3% to 5% of the IPO's gross proceeds, which, in our example, means an investment of between $3 million and $5 million).

3. The underwriters of the IPO defer a portion (often as much as half) of their fees until the SPAC completes its initial business combination.

The insiders' purchase of warrants or units not only increases the dollar amount that can be placed in trust for the benefit of the public stockholders (because the IPO expenses, including the nondeferred portion of the underwriters' compensation, can be paid from the funds obtained from such purchase), it also provides funds for the SPAC to use while seeking a prospective target business and gives greater comfort to the public stockholders by further aligning management's interests with their interests. Since the deferred portion of the underwriters' compensation is paid to the underwriters upon completion of a business combination, such deferral decreases the amount in the trust account available for the combined company if a business combination is not completed.

Unless and until a business combination is completed, the insider stockholders do not have the same liquidity as the SPAC's public stockholders. Unlike the public stockholders, who may trade their shares in the public market or otherwise, insiders are prohibited from selling their securities until at least the completion of the SPAC's initial business combination. Further, if no such transaction is completed within the time period designated, causing the liquidation of the trust account, the insiders are not permitted to participate with the public stockholders in such liquidation, and their shares and warrants (or units) become worthless.

None of the insiders or their affiliates receives any payments for services rendered by them to the SPAC (including salaries or finder's fees), or otherwise, prior to or in connection with the SPAC's initial business combination, other than the nominal payment for office space and related services (generally $7,500 a month) that is typically made to an entity affiliated with the insiders.

At the time of the IPO, some or all of the SPAC's insiders are required to enter into agreements to indemnify the SPAC to the extent claims by third parties reduce the amount available for distribution to the public stockholders if a business combination is not completed and the trust account is liquidated. As a result and as further protection for the public stockholders, a SPAC typically will not do business with a vendor or consider a business combination with a prospective target until the vendor or target executes an agreement waiving any right, title, interest, or claim of any kind it may have against the SPAC's trust account.

Although a SPAC is a very attractive business combination partner, its capital structure, with the "warrant overhang," creates valuation issues for the private company. As described, at the time of the business combination, a SPAC's ratio of warrants to shares is approximately one to one.

SPAC FEATURES RELATING TO A BUSINESS COMBINATION

A SPAC has a limited time period in which to complete its initial business combination. That period may be as short as 18 months to enter into a letter of intent or definitive agreement for a proposed business combination, with an additional 6 months to complete the transaction, and as long as 36 months to complete a business combination. If a business combination is not completed within the prescribed time period, the trust account is liquidated (which may require stockholder approval depending on the structure and governing law).

In addition to applicable stockholder approval requirements imposed by the laws of the jurisdiction in which the SPAC is incorporated, additional requirements are imposed on the SPAC with respect to its completion of a business combination through its charter documents and contractually in the underwriting agreement. Generally, the target company must have a fair value equal to at least 80% of the SPAC's net assets. This does not mean that 80% of the funds in the trust account must be used by the SPAC to pay for the business combination; it is merely a requirement for the minimum value of the target business to be acquired. The SPAC may pay the sellers with cash from the trust account, with monies raised in equity and/or debt financings or with stock, or with any combination of the foregoing.

The business combination must be approved by a majority of the shares actually voted by the public stockholders, and the sponsors are required to vote in accordance with the vote of the public stockholders. In addition, public stockholders receive a second chance to decide whether to maintain their investment in the SPAC at the time the vote for the business combination is taken. Any public stockholder that votes against the business combination may elect at the time of such vote to have its shares converted into its pro rata portion of the proceeds held in the trust account when and if the proposed combination is actually completed. However, if public stockholders holding a number of shares in excess of a specified percentage of the SPAC's public shares elect to exercise their conversion rights, the SPAC is not permitted to proceed with that particular business combination. Historically, a SPAC could not proceed with a business combination if holders of at least 20% of the public shares exercised their conversion rights. A 30% threshold has become more typical, and for some SPACs, the percentage is as high as 40%. What this means is that, if public stockholders holding 30% (for example) of the public shares both vote against the combination and exercise their conversion rights, the SPAC cannot complete the business combination even if public stockholders holding a majority of the public shares have voted in its favor. If, however, holders of less than 30% of the public shares exercise their conversion rights, a majority of the SPAC's shares are voted in favor of the combination, and all of the other conditions to the business combination are met, then the transaction may proceed and, upon its completion, the public stockholders that exercised their conversion rights will receive the portion of the funds held in the trust account relating to their shares and their shares will be canceled.

A SPAC must solicit its public stockholders' approval of the business combination through the proxy statement process. This process is lengthy. The SEC will review and comment on the proxy statement, often creating a period of 120 days or more between the initial filing of the preliminary proxy statement with the SEC and the mailing of the definitive proxy statement to the SPAC's stockholders. If, however, the SPAC is a "foreign private issuer" under the federal securities laws, the stockholder approval process is greatly reduced because filing and review of the proxy statement with and by the SEC is not required. However, SPACs commit to solicit their stockholders' votes through a proxy statement containing the information required by the SEC for U.S. public entities, even if it is not required under the federal securities laws.

Concurrently with the completion of the business combination, the funds held in the trust account, less any funds used to satisfy public stockholder conversion rights, are released to the SPAC, some of which, as discussed earlier, may be used to pay all or a portion of the SPAC's purchase of the acquired business. In connection with the stockholder approval of the business combination, the public stockholders usually are requested to approve changes to the SPAC's charter documents so the provisions specific to the SPAC will cease upon the consummation of the transaction. These provisions typically may be amended only in connection with a business combination, as a further protection for the public stockholders.

The stockholder protections, such as the second-look vote and conversion rights afforded to public stockholders and the limited time period afforded to management to complete a business combination that are the fundamental structure of the SPAC and that attract IPO investors, create serious hurdles to completing the business combination.

BUSINESS COMBINATION PROCESS

From the target's perspective, the business combination process is very different from a business combination with an operating public company. Because of the unique characteristics of a SPAC, the target company must be prepared to invest a lot more time, effort, and money in the process to complete the transaction successfully.

The economics of the SPAC common stock/warrant unit provide a guaranteed return to IPO investors if a business combination is not completed and provide an even greater return to an investor that exercises its conversion rights in connection with a vote against a business combination that is subsequently completed. The IPO investor can sell the warrant included in the unit and reduce its cost basis in the stock to below the per-share amount in the trust. Currently, the per-share amount in a SPAC's trust at the time of the IPO is 100% of the purchase price of the unit sold in the IPO (often 99% to 100% of the IPO price), and the per-share amount in the trust account will continue to rise as interest is earned on the funds held in the SPAC's trust account. As a result, the typical SPAC IPO investor, a hedge fund, can calculate an expected rate of return based on (a) an estimated sale price of the warrant after it becomes separately traded and (b) expected interest rates over the SPAC's term. The earlier in a SPAC's life that a business combination is voted on and expected to be completed, the higher the annualized return is likely to be.

Many of the hedge funds that invest in SPAC IPOs are investing to generate a return rather than to take a risk on the success of the business combination. The economics of the IPO and nature of the IPO investor create a hurdle for the SPAC and its target to overcome to complete a successful transaction, as the investor is predisposed to vote against the transaction and exercise its conversion rights.

Because SPAC securities are relatively thinly traded, almost every SPAC and its target must undertake a road show, similar to an IPO road show, to convince existing stockholders to maintain their investment in the combined company and to attract new investors to buy shares from those investors who would vote against the transaction and exercise their conversion rights. Therefore, investors who do not intend to maintain their investment are likely to achieve a higher return by voting against the transaction and converting their shares into its pro rata portion of the trust account than by selling their shares into the open market. If a number of shares greater than the conversion threshold vote against the business combination and exercise their conversion rights, the SPAC cannot proceed with the transaction. Therefore, the SPAC and the target must replace those investors before the stockholder meeting.

Similar to a business combination with any other public company, after the SPAC has identified a prospective target, it will commence preliminary discussions. At some point in the process, the target company will ask the SPAC to sign a confidentiality agreement. The SPAC will ask the target company to execute a trust fund waiver letter, in which the company waives all rights, title, interest, or claims it may have against the SPAC's trust account. The target must be prepared to sign this letter if it desires to proceed.

Because there is the risk that the SPAC may not receive stockholder approval to complete the transaction, the target company often seeks to require the SPAC to pay its attorneys' and accountants' fees relating to the transaction. The target business must determine if the SPAC has enough cash available outside of the trust account to satisfy any obligation it may incur during the business combination process. If the transaction is completed, there will be one combined company, so it does not matter which party paid the fees. It is a different story, however, if the transaction does not close. If the SPAC agrees to pay the target's fees if the transaction does not occur but does not advance the fees or an estimate thereof or escrow sufficient funds to pay the fees, the target runs the risk that the SPAC will not have the funds available to satisfy its obligations. The SPAC will incur other obligations and make other payments, including to its own attorneys, accountants, and other professionals, during the process. If the transaction proceeds to a stockholder vote and is rejected by the SPAC's stockholders, it will be costly to the SPAC. The SPAC may spend most, if not all, of its cash available outside of the trust during the process. Because the target has waived any claim it may have against the trust, the target can seek to have its obligation satisfied only from funds available outside of the trust, which will have been substantially depleted during the process. Therefore, it is good practice for the target to insist that the SPAC pay its fees and that an estimate of its expenses be escrowed to pay them as they are incurred.

Unless the SPAC identifies the prospective target early, the parties typically will execute a letter of intent rather than proceeding directly to a definitive agreement due to the SPAC's built-in time constraints. If the SPAC has plenty of time to negotiate a definitive agreement, it may elect to proceed directly to that agreement. The SPAC will immediately announce the letter of intent or definitive agreement on a current report on Form 8-K to alert the public that it has satisfied the timing requirement. Once the definitive agreement is executed, a "pregnant Form 8-K" will be filed with the SEC. A pregnant Form 8-K is one that contains more information than is typical for what is being reported, and includes detailed information about the target company as well as about the transaction. This filing may also include road show materials. The purpose of the detailed Form 8-K is to allow the companies to begin to hold meetings with the SPAC's stockholders and prospective investors prior to filing a proxy statement. Although the companies may seek to hold investor meetings prior to the release of the Form 8-K, they can do so only if the investors execute confidentiality agreements. Otherwise, the SPAC would violate Regulation FD of the federal securities laws, which prohibits a public company from disclosing material nonpublic information on a private basis to persons who may trade in the company's securities.

It is suggested that the parties begin the preparation of the SPAC's proxy statement while negotiating the definitive agreement to condense the time between execution of the definitive agreement and the mailing of the proxy statement. The target can expect the SEC to closely scrutinize the proxy statement and focus its questions on the transaction and the target's business. Although the proxy statement is a document filed by the SPAC (or a holding company formed by the SPAC if required by the structure of the transaction or if there is a simultaneous reincorporation merger), the target should expect that it and its attorneys and accountants will be doing the majority of the work on the proxy statement, both to provide the information in the preliminary proxy statement and in response to SEC comments.

During the proxy process, a key indicator of market acceptance or resistance to the transaction is the market price of the SPAC's warrants. Unlike the common stock, which would be converted into the pro rata portion of the trust account, the SPAC's warrants would become worthless if the business combination is not completed. Therefore, a low trading price for the warrants (compared to the warrants' historical market prices prior to the announcement of the transaction or the theoretical value of the warrants under financial formulas, such as the Black-Scholes valuation method) indicates that the market expects the transaction will not be approved.

Once the target company has determined that it may proceed with a potential transaction with a SPAC, it is strongly recommended that it engage an investment banking firm that has expertise in this type of transaction to advise and guide it through the process because of the many unique aspects of the transaction. Because of the uniqueness of the SPAC's structure and the process, particularly the need for a road show and the need to develop a plan to structure potential deals with existing stockholders and potential investors to ensure that the transaction will be approved, experienced investment bankers on both sides of the transaction can be the difference between a successful transaction and a failed one.

The investment bankers will also help to identify the existing SPAC holders, including those that are fundamental holders and potential fundamental buyers. SPAC holders that have already sold their warrants either made their initial investment to achieve their expected return or do not view the transaction favorably. These stockholders must be incentivized to maintain their investment or replaced. In the latter case, they represent blocks of stock available to be placed with potential fundamental buyers. Conversely, those SPAC holders that hold warrants are expected to vote in favor of the transaction and viewed as fundamental holders and potential buyers of additional stock. The investment bankers will help to identify the expected yes and no votes; structure and arrange transactions with SPAC holders to incentivize them to maintain their investment and with fundamental holders to purchase stock; and arrange for sales by those SPAC holders that would otherwise exercise their conversion rights.

GETTING THE VOTE

For all but the best SPAC business combinations, getting the SPAC's stockholder vote and limiting exercises of conversions is by far the most difficult and uncertain part of the process. The uncertainty affects not only whether the transaction will be completed but also the extent to which concessions will be made by the SPAC's sponsors and the target to complete the transaction. The greater the percentage of arbitrageurs holding the SPAC's stock or the less favorably the transaction is perceived, the greater the concessions that will have to be made.

Investment bankers and SPAC sponsors sometimes seek to avoid or minimize this problem at the time of the IPO by imposing certain requirements upon the SPAC's sponsors, such as:

- **Rule 10b5-1 trading plans.** SPAC sponsors may enter into Rule 10b5-1 trading plans prior to the effective date of the IPO. Such plans require them to purchase up to specified number of shares or dollar amount of shares at the prevailing market prices. The plans provide a specified maximum price at which purchase would be made. The maximum price is set at or slightly above the expected per-share amount in the SPAC's trust account at the time a stockholder vote would occur. These purchases are intended to support the market price of the stock. They provide potential sellers the ability to dispose of their shares and achieve the same or a greater return than if they were to vote against the transaction and exercise their conversion rights. These purchases are made during the proxy process to avoid issues under Regulation M under the Securities Act of 1933 and must be made in accordance with Rule 10b-18 under that act to avoid market manipulation issues.

- **Agreements to buy securities from the SPAC simultaneously with the completion of the business combination.** SPAC sponsors may commit to purchase the combined company's securities directly from the company simultaneously with the completion of the business combination. These agreements would be entered into prior to the effective date of the IPO and would commit the insiders to purchase a specified number of shares or units at a preestablished price, typically the offering price of the unit in the IPO. These agreements may be viewed unfavorably by the market, because if the transaction is favorably received, the stock trades higher and the sponsors will be purchasing securities at a discount to the market price at the time of the transaction.

In most transactions, however, negotiations and deals need to occur during the proxy process because at the time of the IPO, it is not possible to foresee all of the variables involved in the business combination that will affect how much stock will need to be turned over from no votes to yes votes. At the time of the IPO, the actual business combination is not known so market sentiment cannot be estimated. Also, market conditions may change radically between the IPO and the vote on the business combination, as many SPACs learned in 2007 and the first quarter of 2008. An IPO investor that initially was thought to be a fundamental investor may not be one at the time of the vote. Therefore, SPAC sponsors may commit to these strategies in advance of the proxy process without any guarantee that they will achieve their purpose and may commit to spend funds to buy stock in the open market that can be better targeted during the proxy process.

Many different transactions can be entered into during the proxy process all the way up through the closing of the business combination that have been negotiated with existing SPAC stockholders and new investors to obtain approval of the transaction. The target's owners may be required to make certain concessions in order to get the transaction completed. The SPAC's sponsor may not be willing to give up enough equity to satisfy the SPAC's stockholders or provide stock price guarantees to the SPAC's stockholders after the transaction because they will not be running the company. Additionally, public stockholders may require concessions on a larger scale, such as reducing the purchase price, deferring a portion of the purchase price, or making a portion of the purchase price contingent on preference. At that point, the target's owners are forced to consider renegotiating their original deal or having the deal rejected by the SPAC's stockholders. Different incentives used to support a proposed transaction include:

- **Purchases by the SPAC sponsors in the open market.** The SPAC sponsors may make open market purchases to help support the price of the SPAC's stock to enable those who would vote against the transaction to find selling their shares more attractive. A concern with this practice is that the sponsors subject themselves to claims under Rule 10b-5 of the Securities Act of 1933 for trading on material nonpublic information, even though the proxy statement should contain all material information relating to the SPAC, the target, and the transaction. Additionally, all purchases must be made in compliance with Rule 10b-18 under the Securities Act to avoid potential market manipulation issues.

- **Sponsors forfeit a portion of their equity.** By forfeiting a portion of their equity, the sponsors are reducing the dilution to the public stockholders and effectively reducing the cost of the transaction.

- **Sponsors transfer a portion of their equity to other SPAC stockholders.** The SPAC stockholders may be incentivized to maintain their investment by increasing their potential return. The negotiation centers around how much additional equity the arbitrageur will require; typically it is a function of how these holders expect the stock to trade post-combination.

- **Grants of put options.** A put option is a stock price guarantee settled in either cash or stock by requiring the party granting the put option to purchase a specified number of shares at a specified price on a specified date. In the Paramount Acquisition Corp./B.J.K. Inc. (aka Chem/RX) combination, the principals of the target company granted put options to existing SPAC stockholders and to investors who agreed to purchase stock of the SPAC. The target's principals escrowed approximately $34 million of the proceeds they received to satisfy this potential obligation and have the ability to settle their obligation, if the shares are put to them, either by purchasing the shares at the put price or by paying the holders of the shares the difference between the put price and the price at which the stockholders are able to sell their shares. In connection with the Aldabra 2 Acquisition Corp./Boise Cascade combination, certain principals of the target company granted contingent value rights to 40 institutional stockholders of the Aldabra 2 SPAC to incentivize them to support the transaction. The holders of these rights may exercise them during a one-week period of time after the first anniversary of the transaction if the company's stock does not achieve an average trading price of $10.50 during the 30 days prior to such period. The principals would be required to pay the holders up to $1.00 per share in cash, stock, or a combination.

• **Renegotiate or restructure the purchase price.** A renegotiation or restructuring of the transaction could involve a substantial reduction in the purchase price the target's owners would receive. A renegotiation might mean that some of the cash or equity the target's owners would have received at the closing would be deferred or would become subject to the company satisfying certain preference targets. In the Chem/RX transaction mentioned, the terms of the combination were amended to provide that $15 million of the cash consideration that would have been initially payable to Chem/RX's stockholders would become contingent and payable in the future if performance milestones were achieved.

Any specifically negotiated deal must be publicly disclosed promptly so that the SPAC's stockholders will have time to consider the transaction prior to voting on the transaction at the SPAC's stockholders meeting. The SPAC must file a current report on Form 8-K and/or additional definitive proxy-soliciting materials with the SEC to make the proper disclosures.

At the time the definitive agreement is executed, the target's owners must be prepared to make concessions to obtain the vote and should negotiate with the SPAC's sponsors regarding how each party's economic obligations to incentivize existing SPAC stockholders and potential purchasers of the SPAC's stock would be allocated if the need arises.

THE GOOD, THE BAD, AND THE REJECTED

The management team of a SPAC is highly incentivized to complete the best deal it can. The SPAC's founders hold a 20% interest in the common stock of the SPAC and typically hold warrants to purchase additional equity as well. The better the business combination, the better the combined company's stock should perform and the greater their profit. However, many management teams do not negotiate an ideal transaction, for a number of reasons:

- They do not come across one.
- Due to errors in judgment.
- There is insufficient time to complete the diligence.
- They are forced to overpay for a target business because of competition for a target or lack of time to find another target.

With a lesser-quality deal, as long as the SPAC's stockholders approve the transaction, the SPAC's founders may still make a considerable amount of money, even if the stock trades down. A "bad deal" for the SPAC may, at first, look like a good deal for the target's owners because the purchase price for their company may be acceptable. However, if the owners are receiving a large portion of their consideration in the form of stock, their good deal can very easily turn bad if the stock does not perform well because of a perceived overvaluation by the public markets or otherwise. Also, both the SPAC's management team and the target's owners have to be concerned that a perceived bad deal for the SPAC will be rejected or require significant concessions or restructuring to satisfy the SPAC's stockholders. From the SPAC's perspective, if it goes through the proxy process and its stockholders vote against the transaction, it may not have the time necessary to identify another prospective target or complete another transaction and will be forced to liquidate.

The Good

Good deals are business combinations with a quality business, valued at a healthy multiple of the amount held in the SPAC's trust account, and fairly valued and structured to overcome the SPAC's structural limitations. Target company attributes that will help support the success of the announcement of a transaction are:

- High-profile company
- Availability of substantial cash post-combination to help the combined company achieve growth (i.e., not all of the SPAC's trust account will be used to pay the acquisition price)
- Target's strong growth potential—cumulative annual growth and earnings before interest, taxes, depreciation, and amortization (EBITDA) above industry or sector averages
- A successful strategy with significant expansion potential
- Target's willingness to accept a fairly priced transaction rather than holding out for maximum value (The SPAC must leverage the dilution of the sponsors' equity, and pricing a transaction fairly helps to achieve that goal.)

For a transaction to be successful, the market must perceive the business combination positively, as evidenced by the SPAC's stock trading above its liquidation value (i.e., the per-share amount in the trust account), and the post-transaction operating companies must continue to perform.

The GLG Partners business combination with Freedom Acquisition Holdings, Inc. was a model business combination. Freedom went public in December 2006 by selling units, consisting of one share and one warrant exercisable at $7.50 per share. Its sponsors included Nicolas Berggruen and Martin Franklin, each of whom has well-established representations for buying, selling, and operating companies. The sponsors received 12 million units (identical to those units sold to the public) for $25,000 and also purchased 4.5 million warrants (identical to the warrants included in the units sold to the public) at a price of $1.00 per warrant. The sponsors also agreed to invest $50 million in the company upon completion of the business combination by purchasing 5 million units at $10 per unit.

Freedom had approximately $519 million in its trust account, 64.8 million shares outstanding, and warrants to purchase 69.3 million shares outstanding on June 25, 2007, when it announced it had entered into an agreement to acquire GLG, a $23 billion hedge fund, for consideration consisting of $1 billion in cash and 230 million shares of common stock and common stock equivalents. The structure of this transaction was ideal for a SPAC because the valuation of the company it acquired was five to six times the amount it held in trust. Since the SPAC's management paid only a nominal amount for its equity, the greater the multiplied value of the target to the SPAC, the less dilutive the SPAC management's interest would be to the combined company. Additionally, the issuance, in this case, of approximately four times as many shares to the target company as payment of the merger consideration further reduced the dilutive effect of the management interest and of the below-market exercise price of the warrants. The public markets viewed the transaction favorably, as the stock closed at $11.18 and $13.70 respectively on the date of the announcement of the definitive agreement and the closing of the acquisition. GLG's securities continue to perform well, providing a return of over approximately 90% to Freedom's IPO investors as of March 2008.

For GLG, the transaction was an efficient way to obtain capital without having to incur the burden and risk of undertaking its own IPO. GLG's original stockholders returned a nearly 75% ownership in the combined company.

For Freedom's sponsors, as of April 1, 2008, their $25,000 investment was worth approximately $200 million, and their warrant and unit investments were worth over $100 million.

The Bad

Bad deals are business combinations that trade below the trust's per share amount after announcement, require restructuring or renegotiation, or require the SPAC's sponsors or the target's owners to enter into other agreements to incentivize the SPAC's public stockholders or potential investors to support the transaction and trade poorly after the transaction. None of the parties fares well in a bad deal, other than possibly the SPAC sponsors. Because the SPAC sponsors' purchase price for 20% of the SPAC's equity is only nominal, even poor performance by the post-combination company can result in a profit for the sponsors. However, the equity of the SPAC's sponsors would be worth considerably less than they expected because of the decline in the stock price, which may be coupled with a reduced equity stake. The institutional investors lose because the incentives they receive do not cover the loss in value of their stock, and the value of the target's owners' consideration is greatly reduced as a result of the decline in the stock price and the concessions they make.

The Aldabra 2/Boise combination completed in February 2008 showed all of the signs of being a bad deal only two months later. The transaction was first announced in September 2007. Aldabra 2's stock continued to trade at a substantial discount to the per-share amount held in the trust account. Less than one week before the Aldabra 2 stockholders' meeting, the principals of Boise granted contingent value rights to 40 institutional stockholders of Aldabra 2, agreeing to pay an amount equal to the difference in between $10.50 and the market price of the company's stock one year after the combination, based on a specified formula, up to $1.00 per share. On the date the transaction was announced, the stock closed at $9.56, below the reported $9.789 per share that was distributed to holders that exercised conversion rights. Just two months later, the company's stock traded as low as $5.25.

The Sand Hill IT Security Acquisition Corp./St. Bernard Software, Inc. business combination is an even more extreme example of a bad deal. The proposed transaction was first announced in October 2005. Sand Hill's stock began to trade lower after the announcement. Prior to the announcement, the stock traded above the reported per-share amount in the trust account of $5.24; thereafter, the stock price dropped to $5.15, below the per-share amount in the trust account. Upon completion of the business combination in July 2006, the combined company's stock traded at $5.09, below the reported $5.40 per share distributed to those Sand Hill stockholders that voted against the transaction and elected to convert their shares into their portion of the trust account. Since the business combination, St. Bernard's stock has been very illiquid and has continued to decline dramatically, trading below the $0.50 in the third quarter of 2008. The SPAC's sponsor's equity, theoretically worth $50 million before the business combination, was worth less than $5 million in early 2008. The $50 million of stock issued to St. Bernard's stockholders in the business combination was worth less than $5 million in August 2008.

The Rejected

A rejected deal usually means the end of the SPAC. The SPAC's certificate of incorporation provides for a specified time frame in which a business combination must be completed and, more important, in which the SPAC must enter into a letter of intent or definitive agreement for a business combination. Because the stockholder approval process is lengthy, if a potential transaction is rejected by the SPAC's stockholders, in all but rare cases, the SPAC will run out of time to complete another transaction and be forced to liquidate at its deadline. For the SPAC's sponsors, their investment in the SPAC will be worthless and their reputations for completing acquisitions will be greatly tarnished.

The number of rejected business combinations has increased regularly since the first liquidation of a SPAC was announced in the third quarter of 2006. As of September 1, 2008, of the 159 SPACs that had completed their IPOs, 20 SPACs liquidated or announced that they were liquidating or that their proposed business combinations were rejected. Oracle Healthcare Acquisition Corp., Harbor Acquisition Corp., and HD Partners Acquisition Corp. are three SPACs that announced that their acquisition agreements were terminated in 2008. Of these three, only HD's business combination was rejected at a formal vote of its stockholders. On the day prior to its scheduled vote, Harbor's target terminated the transaction because proxies received by Harbor's stockholders indicated that the transaction would not be approved and the 20% threshold for conversions would be exceeded.

Oracle Healthcare's management agreed to forfeit $15 million of their sponsor's equity, and the target's owners agreed to reduce the consideration paid at closing and accept a portion of their consideration as a contingent payment based on satisfaction of performance targets before the merger agreement was mutually terminated on the day before Oracle Healthcare's scheduled stockholder meeting, due to currently prevailing market considerations. In each of these transactions, the initial investment of the SPAC's sponsors was between $1.3 million and $2.25 million, and became worthless upon liquidation.

The target also feels the adverse consequences. First, it will have spent a great deal of time, resources, and money to complete the transaction. The HD Partners business combination was first announced in May 2007 and terminated in February 2008. The target devoted almost one year to this transaction. The target may have also rejected other possible transactions and not been able to focus on business developments and opportunities, instead focusing on completing the business combination. After the SPAC's stockholders have rejected the transaction, information about the proposed transaction will become publicly available and other potential holders will know what the target's owners were willing to accept to sell the company. For example, Precision Therapeutic Inc., Oracle Healthcare's target, publicly announced that it agreed to accept reduced consideration and accept a sizable portion of the consideration on a contingent basis upon satisfaction of performance criteria. Additionally, the target will have made extensive disclosures about its business that it had not historically made—and would not have wanted made as a private company—which could place it at a competitive disadvantage as a private company.

NOTE

1. The New York Stock Exchange SPAC rules were approved by the SEC in Release No. 34-57785, May 6, 2008.

Chapter 14

Regulation A: $5 Million Offering

Regulation A is an exemption from registration requirements of the Securities Act of 1933. Complying with Regulation A does not exempt the company from having to meet state securities law requirements. Do not assume that because the company has qualified its offering under Regulation A, the company can sell its securities in any state it wants. There is little comfort in being arrested by the state police instead of the FBI.

Regulation A offerings are exempt from federal registration but not from Securities and Exchange Commission (SEC) review. The company must submit an offering circular to the SEC for review. The company must wait for comments and comply with such comments prior to the SEC declaring the offering statement effective. In this respect, there is very little difference between a traditional initial public offering (IPO) registered with the SEC and a Regulation A offering. The primary advantages of a Regulation A over a traditional registered offering are:

- The company can test the waters prior to going to the expense of preparing the offering statement (where permitted by state law).

- Audited financial statements are not required for federal review, unless otherwise available. (However, states may still require audited financials to satisfy state securities laws.)
- Less disclosure is required.
- The company can use a question-and-answer format in the offering circular.

TESTING THE WATERS

The major advantage of the Regulation A offering is that the company can determine if there is any investor interest prior to incurring significant legal, accounting, and printing costs. Unlike a registered offering, the company may solicit indications of interest prior to preparing or filing a Regulation A offering statement with the SEC.

This testing-the-waters rule permits the company to publish or deliver a simple written document or make a scripted radio or television broadcast to determine if there is investor interest. The company can say anything it wishes in the test-the-waters document or script, with two exceptions:

- The document or script cannot violate the antifraud laws.
- The document or script must contain certain required disclosures.

The written document or script of the broadcast must identify the chief executive officer of the company and identify briefly and in general its business and products. The document or script must also state that no money is being solicited and, if sent, will not be accepted. Moreover, the document or script must state that an indication of interest involves no obligation or commitment of any kind by the investor and that no sales will be made until a completed offering circular is delivered.

The inability to legally bind investors, or even to escrow their money, is a serious drawback to the utility of the test-the-waters rule. A period of three or more months may pass between the date the investors express their interest until the date the complete offering circular has cleared the SEC and become available for distribution. Investors who initially express an interest in the investment may change their minds in the interim.

The utility of using radio, television, or newspaper marketing is also questionable. Traditionally, securities are sold by personal recommendation of brokers, friends, barbers, and the like. Investors typically follow these recommendations because they are theoretically given privately to the proposed customer. The customer has a sense of being favored with exclusive information not available to the public. The public nature of radio, television, or newspaper marketing may detract from the investor appeal of the company's securities.

Despite these handicaps, the ability to solicit indications of interest without incurring major expense can be very useful. The rule permits any written document provided to the potential investor to contain a coupon, returnable to the company. The coupon would reveal the name, address, and telephone number of the prospective investor. This permits the accumulation of a potential investor list, which can be useful after the offering circular has cleared the SEC.

Once the company submits the written document or script to the SEC, the company can orally communicate with the potential investor. This permits a sales pitch by telephone. Obviously, all communications are subject to the antifraud provisions of federal and state securities laws.

Any solicitation to purchase a security must satisfy state as well as federal securities laws. The company must check with the state in which any offer is to be made to see if testing the waters is legal. If an investor who lives in Michigan is vacationing in Maine when the company solicits the investor, it must check securities laws of both Michigan and Maine.

Apart from testing-the-waters rules, the rules relating to when offers and sales of securities under a Regulation A offering may be made are similar to those applicable to a traditional IPO.

WHO CAN FILE UNDER REGULATION A?

The major requirements for any company that wishes to file a Regulation A offering statement are listed next.

- The company must be organized in the United States or Canada.
- The company must not be a public company. (It must not file reports under Section 13 or 15(d) of the Securities Exchange Act of 1934.)
- The company must not be a development-stage company that either has no specific business plan or purpose or has indicated that its business plan is to merge with an unidentified company.

It should be noted that development-stage companies that do have a specific business plan (other than merging with some unidentified company) do qualify for Regulation A.

BAD BOY DISQUALIFICATION

Rule 262 of Regulation A contains a "bad boy" provision disqualifying certain companies from filing under Regulation A. The provision is waivable by the SEC upon a showing of good cause. The bad boy provision is very broad and denies use of Regulation A in these situations, among others:

- If any director, officer, 10% shareholder, promoter, underwriter, or any partner, director, or officer of an underwriter:
  - Was convicted within 10 years prior to filing of certain felonies or misdemeanors relating generally to securities
  - Is subject to a court, SEC, or U.S. postal service order enjoining certain activities relating to securities or use of the mails to make false representations
  - Is suspended or expelled from membership in certain securities associations

- If the company, or any of its predecessors, or any affiliated issuer, or any underwriter have had certain problems with the SEC or others within the past five years

HOW MUCH MONEY CAN BE RAISED?

The company may raise a maximum of $5 million in cash and other consideration under Regulation A within a 12-month period. In computing the $5 million figure, the company must subtract the aggregate offering price for all securities sold within 12 months before the start of the Regulation A offering. Thus, the company may raise a maximum of $5 million every 12 months (plus the time necessary to offer and sell the securities).

Regulation A also permits the receipt of up to $1.5 million in cash or other consideration by all selling security holders. However, the company may not make affiliate resales if it has not had net income from continuing operations in at least one of its last two fiscal years.

The company must subtract the amount sold by selling security holders in computing the $5 million limit. Thus, if selling security holders sell $1.5 million of their securities, the company can sell only $3.5 million during the relevant 12-month period.

There are complicated rules for computing the $5 million limit, particularly the "integration" rules. For example, securities sold in a private placement within six months after the completion of the Regulation A offering may have to be integrated with the Regulation A, thereby destroying the exemption. An experienced securities lawyer can assist the company in navigating these complicated rules.

OFFERING STATEMENT AND OFFERING CIRCULAR

The company files a Regulation A offering statement with the SEC's national office in Washington, DC. The Regulation A offering statement is analogous to a registration statement for a traditional registered offering. The Regulation A offering circular is analogous to the prospectus, which the company would include in a registration statement for a traditional registered offering.

The offering circular must include a balance sheet as of the end of the most recent fiscal year and statements of income, cash flows, and other stockholders' equity for each of the two fiscal years preceding the date of the balance sheet. The company must prepare financial statements in accordance with generally accepted accounting principles in the United States, but these do not need to be audited. However, if audited financial statements are available, the company must provide them.

The company has the option of preparing the offering circular in a question-and-answer format. If the company has audited financial statements and does not need to test the waters, it should consider the alternative of filing a Form S-1. The use of a Form S-1, which registers securities under the Securities Act of 1933 (versus the Regulation A exemption), may actually make it easier to qualify the offering under state securities laws.

OUTLINE OF REGULATION A

The following is a more detailed outline of Regulation A:

A. Overview

1. This regulation grants an exemption from the registration provisions of the 1933 Act for public offerings of securities of no more than $5 million in a 12-month period, including no more than $1.5 million in non-issuer resales.

2. The nonfinancial portions of the Regulation A offering circular, which is included in the Regulation A offering statement, can be prepared in a question-and-answer format.

3. Except as provided by the test-the-waters provisions, no offers may be made until a Regulation A offering statement is filed

with the SEC and no sales may be made until the offering statement has been qualified and an offering circular is delivered.

4. Pursuant to the test-the-waters provisions, an issuer may obtain indications of interest in a proposed offering prior to filing an offering statement; however, no solicitation or acceptance of money nor any commitment to purchase is permitted until the offering statement is qualified. Copies of any written document must be submitted to the SEC.

5. The company and its controlling persons remain liable for material misstatements and omissions in the offering statement or the offering circular.

B. Issuer and Offering Requirements

1. The issuer:

   a. Must be organized in the United States or Canada

   b. Must be neither a reporting company nor an investment company

   c. Must not be a development-stage company that either has no specific business plan or purpose, or has indicated that its business plan is to merge with an unidentified company or companies

   d. May not be issuing fractional undivided interests in oil or gas rights or similar interests in other mineral rights

   e. Must not be disqualified because of administrative or court orders as set forth in Rule 262

   Note: Rule 262 provides that if the issuer, any of its predecessors or any affiliated issuer, any of its directors, officers, general partners, or 10% equity owners, any promoter, any underwriter or partner, director, or officer of such underwriter are subject to certain specified civil, criminal, or administrative actions, the exemption provided by Regulation A will not be available. The Rule provides that the SEC, upon a showing of good cause, may waive the disqualification provisions.

2. The aggregate amount offered and sold in reliance on the Regulation A exemption may not exceed $5 million in any 12-month period. Not more than $1.5 million of such amount may be offered and sold by selling security holders and no affiliate resales are permitted if the issuer has not had net income from continuing operations in at least one of its last two fiscal years.

    a. In computing the aggregate amount offered, offers and sales made in the preceding 12 months not in reliance on Regulation A need not be included.

    b. If securities are offered for both cash and noncash consideration, the offering price should be based on the cash price. If the securities are not offered for cash, the offering price should be based on the value of consideration as established by bona fide sales of that consideration or, in the absence of sales, on the fair value as determined by an accepted standard.

3. Integration

    a. There is a specific safe-harbor provision relating to integration that states that offers and sales made in reliance on Regulation A will not be integrated with any prior offers or sales. It further provides that there will be no integration with subsequent offers or sales that are (1) registered under the 1933 Act, (2) made in reliance on Rule 701 (stock option plans and certain other compensatory benefit plans) or Regulation S (foreign sales), (3) made pursuant to an employee benefit plan, or (4) made more than six months after the Regulation A offering is completed.

    b. If the safe-harbor rule does not apply to particular offers or sales, such offers and sales still may not be integrated, depending upon the particular facts and circumstances. See Securities Act Release No. 4552 (November 6, 1962).

C. Offers Prior to and After Filing and Qualification of Offering Statement

    1. Prior to Filing; Test-the-Waters Rule

a. Prior to the filing of the offering statement, an issuer may publish or deliver a written document or make scripted radio or television broadcasts to determine whether there is any interest in the securities intended to be offered. A copy of this document should be submitted to the SEC's main office in Washington, DC (Attn: Office of Small Business Review).

b. The written document or script of the broadcast must:

(1) State that no money or other consideration is being solicited and, if sent in response, will not be accepted.

(2) State that no sales of the securities will be made or commitment to purchase accepted until delivery of an offering circular that includes complete information about the issuer and the offering.

(3) State that an indication of interest made by a prospective investor involves no obligation or commitment of any kind.

(4) Identify the chief executive officer of the issuer and identify briefly and in general its business and products:

(a) No sales may be made until 20 days after the last publication or delivery of the document or radio or television broadcast.

(b) Any written document may include a coupon, returnable to the issuer, indicating interest in a potential offering.

(c) If an issuer has a bona fide change of intention and decides to register an offering after using the test-the-waters process, it must wait at least 30 days before filing a registration statement with the SEC.

2. After Filing and Before Qualification: After seven copies of the offering statement have been filed with the SEC's office in Washington, DC, the following activities are permissible:

a. Oral offers may be made and copies of the preliminary offering circular may be delivered to prospective investors. The preliminary offering circular must be clearly marked as such, must contain substantially the same information as the final offering circular, and must indicate that no securities may be sold until a final offering circular is delivered.

b. Advertisements indicating only (1) the name of the issuer,(2) the amount being offered and the offering price, (3) the general type of the issuer's business, and (4) the general character and location of its property may be used, if they state from whom an offering circular may be obtained.

3. After Qualification: After the offering statement has been qualified, oral offers and written offers, if accompanied or preceded by an offering circular, may be made if a preliminary or final offering circular is furnished to the purchaser at least 48 hours prior to the mailing of the confirmation and a final offering circular is delivered with the confirmation, unless it has previously been delivered.

D. Information Required to Be Disclosed in Offering Circular

1. The offering circular must include a balance sheet as of the end of the most recent fiscal year and statements of income, cash flows, and other stockholders' equity for each of the two fiscal years preceding the date of the balance sheet.

2. For nonfinancial disclosure, the issuer may choose from three options:

a. A question-and-answer format substantially similar to the SCOR (small corporate offering registration) document (also called Form U-7) used by many states to register securities for small offerings may be used by a corporate issuer.

b. The traditional Regulation A format, which is similar to a prospectus used in a registered offering, may be used by any issuer.

c. Any issuer may choose to furnish the information required by Part I of Form SB-2.

3. The offering circular, which is a part of the offering statement, must include the narrative and financial information required by

Form 1-A in a clear, concise, and understandable manner, and the cover page of every offering circular must include a legend indicating the SEC has not passed upon the merits or given its approval to any securities offered.

4. The offering circular must be signed by the issuer, its chief executive officer, chief financial officer, a majority of the members of its board of directors, and any selling security holder.

5. Where the offering circular is distributed through electronic media, issues may satisfy legibility requirements applicable to printed documents by presenting all required information in a format readily communicated to investors.

E. Filing and Qualification of Offering Statement
An offering statement is qualified without SEC action 20 days after filing, unless a delaying notification is included providing that it must be qualified only by order of the SEC.

F. Sales
No sale of securities can be made until:

1. The Form 1-A offering statement has been qualified.

2. A preliminary offering circular or final offering is furnished to the prospective purchaser at least 48 hours prior to the mailing of the confirmation of sale to that person.

3. A final offering circular is delivered to the purchaser with the confirmation of sale, unless it has been delivered to that person at an earlier time.

G. Sales Material and Subsequent Reports Regarding Sales and Use of Proceeds

1. Advertisements and other sales material may be used as indicated in Section C of this outline. Copies of such material should be filed with the office of the SEC where the offering statement was filed when the material is first published or delivered.

2. The issuer should report information concerning the amount of securities sold and the use of proceeds every six months after the offering statement has been qualified until substantially all

of the proceeds have been applied or within 30 days after the completion of the offering, whichever is the latest event.

H. Substantial Good Faith Compliance Defense

   1. Rule 260 provides that a failure to comply with a term, condition, or requirement of Regulation A will not result in the loss of the exemption for any offer or sale to a particular individual, if the person relying on the exemption establishes:

   a. The condition violated was not intended to protect the complaining individual.

   b. The failure to comply was insignificant to the offering as a whole (issuer requirements, aggregate offering limitations, and the requirements to file an offering statement and deliver an offering circular are always significant to the offering as a whole).

   c. A good faith and reasonable attempt was made to comply with all of the requirements of Regulation A.

   2. Rule 260 preserves the SEC's right to pursue any failure in compliance, regardless of significance.

Chapter 15

SCOR: $1 Million Do-It-Yourself Registered Offering

Most states, officially or unofficially, permit the use of a simplified question-and-answer format to register securities under state securities laws when raising funds pursuant to Securities and Exchange Commission (SEC) Rule 504, Regulation A, or so-called intrastate offerings.

This simplified form is the SCOR form (small corporate offering registration) or Form U-7 (also known as ULOR, or uniform limited offering registration). It is also called Registration Form U-7.

The purpose of the SCOR form is to reduce the legal and accounting costs of preparing extensively documented reports. In general, the SCOR form has been praised as being user friendly. Many corporate executives have filed this form without incurring significant outside professional costs.

After the SCOR registration is effective, the company generally may solicit investors, whether they are accredited investors or not. Upon completion of the SCOR offering, a trading market can develop. This contrasts with the accredited investor offering, in which most states that have adopted this exemption do not permit trading for at least a year.

The states, in conjunction with the American Bar Association's State Regulation of Securities Committee, developed the SCOR offering to facilitate raising capital by small businesses. The SCOR offering permits a company to raise up to $1 million within approximately 12 months without federal review of the offering documents. It requires only a state or a regional review.

Theoretically, the small businessperson can respond to the SCOR question-and-answer format himself or herself, or with the advice of a general legal practitioner, and does not need the assistance of a securities law specialist. The SCOR form is then filed with the state or states in which the securities are to be sold.

This theory is somewhat questionable since the SCOR form is not exempt from the antifraud provisions of federal and state securities laws. These antifraud provisions can impose personal liability on the control persons of the company, including its directors and officers.

In addition, the SCOR form contains a number of sophisticated questions that may be beyond the knowledge of the company's officers or their general counsel. For example, question 117 of the form states:

> Describe any other material factors, either adverse or favorable, that will or could affect the Company or its business or which are necessary to make any other information in this Disclosure Document not misleading or incomplete.

The answer to this question requires a knowledge of what facts or circumstances the courts view as "material." Small business owners proceed at their own peril if they try to answer these questions without the assistance of a securities law specialist. It should also be noted that both federal and state securities laws provide for criminal sanctions for flagrant violations.

In light of these considerations, some companies are using sophisticated law firms to help prepare the SCOR form.

It is true, however, that the exemption of the SCOR offering from federal registration by Rule 504 (discussed in the next section) helps minimize the costs of the offering. Also, the practice in this area has evolved into a system where state examiners play a large role in assisting companies with their SCOR document. State regional review of the SCOR document permits review and comment by only one state even though the offering is made in several states.

FEDERAL REGISTRATION EXEMPTION

Rule 504 under the Securities Act of 1933 provides an exemption from the registration provisions of federal law for certain offerings up to $1 million. The registration exemption, however, does not also exempt the offering from the antifraud and personal liability provisions of the law (as noted previously).

Rule 504 permits a qualified nonpublic company to raise up to $1 million, less the aggregate offering price of all securities sold by the company within 12 months before the start of and during the Rule 504 offering (subject to certain exceptions). Rule 504 does not require any specific disclosure to be made, and the offering circulars (prospectuses) are not subject to federal regulatory review.

More important, SEC Rule 504 does not prohibit a general solicitation of investors to market the offering if a SCOR registration is required or if the state permits a general solicitation of accredited investors, provided that the general solicitation is limited to such states (subject to certain exceptions). Thus, after a SCOR registration, marketing may be accomplished by cold telephone calls and radio, television, and newspaper advertising without violating the registration provisions of the 1933 Act. This contrasts with the marketing of private placements that prohibit general solicitations.

Of course, the company must satisfy the requirements of state securities laws before the use of a general solicitation. However, if the company's state requires a SCOR registration, the states generally prohibit any general solicitation prior to the clearance of the SCOR form.

This contrasts with the Rule 504/accredited investor offering, which permits general solicitation of accredited investors without prior clearance from state regulators.[1]

The company must file a Form D with the SEC not later than 15 days after the first sale of securities. The date of filing is the date on which the business mails the notice by registered or certified mail to the SEC's principal office in Washington, DC, or the date the SEC otherwise receives it.

STATE SECURITIES LAWS

Although Rule 504 does not require any specific disclosure to investors, most state securities laws do.

ELIGIBILITY TO USE SCOR

Registrations covered in the SCOR Policy Statement dated April 28, 1996, must meet these requirements.[2] The issuer must

- Be a corporation or centrally managed limited liability company organized under the law of the United States or Canada, or any state, province, or territory or possession thereof, or the District of Columbia, and have its principal place of business in one of the foregoing.
- Not be subject to the reporting requirements of Section 13 or 15(d) of the Securities Exchange Act of 1934.
- Not be an investment company registered or required to be registered under the Investment Company Act of 1940.
- Not be engaged in or propose to be engaged in petroleum exploration and production, mining, or other extractive industries.
- Not be a development stage company that either has no specific business plan or purpose or has indicated that its business plan is to engage in merger or acquisition with an unidentified company or companies or other entity or person.

- Not be disqualified under Section IV of the Policy Statement. [Not reproduced]

- The offering price for common stock or common ownership interests (hereinafter, collectively referred to as common stock), the exercise price for options, warrants or rights to common stock, or the conversion price for securities convertible into common stock must be greater than or equal to U.S. $1.00 per share or unit of interest. The issuer must agree with the Administrator that it will not split its common stock, or declare a stock dividend for two years after the effective date of the registration if such action has the effect of lowering the price below U.S. $1.00.

- Commissions, fees, or other remuneration for soliciting any prospective purchaser in connection with the offering in the state are paid only to persons who, if required to be registered or licensed, the issuer believes, and has reason to believe, are appropriately registered or licensed in the state.

- Financial statements must be prepared in accordance with either U.S. or Canadian generally accepted accounting principles. If appropriate, a reconciliation note should be provided. If the Company has not conducted significant operations, statements of receipts and disbursements shall be included in lieu of statements of income. Interim financial statements may be unaudited. All other financial statements must be audited by independent certified public accountants, provided, however, that if each of the following four conditions are met, such financial statements in lieu of being audited may be reviewed by independent certified public accountants in accordance with the Accounting and Review Service Standards promulgated by the American Institute of Certified Public Accountants or the Canadian equivalent:

  Test 1. The Company shall not have previously sold securities through an offering involving the general solicitation of prospective investors by means of advertising, mass mailing, public meetings, "cold call" telephone solicitation, or any other method directed toward the public;

Test 2. The Company has not been previously required under federal, state, provincial, or territorial securities laws to provide audited financial statements in connection with any sale of its securities;

Test 3. The aggregate amount of all previous sales of securities by the Company (exclusive of debt financing with banks and similar commercial lenders) shall not exceed U.S. $1,000,000; and

Test 4. The amount of the present offering does not exceed U.S. $1,000,000.

• The offering must be made in compliance with Rule 504 of Regulation D, Regulation A, or Rule 147 (intrastate offering) of the Securities Act of 1933. The issuer must comply with the General Instructions to SCOR in Part I of the NASAL SCOR Issuer's Manual.

OFFERS AND SALES

The business cannot offer or sell securities pursuant to the SCOR offering until the state declares the registration effective. The business cannot make pre-effective offers under the SCOR offering form. Thus, there is no testing the waters, as with Regulation A.

ESCROW

If the proposed business of the company requires a minimum amount of proceeds to commence business, the SCOR form requires an escrow of all proceeds received from investors until the company raises the minimum amount. The escrow must be with a bank or a savings and loan association or other similar depository institution.

The Regulation A offering does not require an escrow. However, state securities officials could still require such an escrow under the Regulation A offering in order to permit offers and sales in a particular state.

INSTRUCTIONS AND FORM

Form U-7, which contains the SCOR form, was adopted in 1999. Form U-7 and a helpful Issuer's Manual can be downloaded from the Web site of the North American Securities Administrators Association (www.nasaa.org).

The Web site also contains other useful information. Note that the SCOR form and the Regulation A question-and-answer form are very similar. In fact, the Regulation A question-and-answer form was based in part on the SCOR form. State securities administrators are available to assist companies in filling out Form U-7.

NOTES

1. A number of states permit a company to generally solicit accredited investors under SEC Rule 504 without using a registered agent and without registering the securities being offered:

   • Any natural person whose individual net worth, or joint net worth with that person's spouse, at the time of his purchase exceeds $1 million.

   • Any natural person who had an individual income in excess of $200,000 in each of the two most recent years or joint income with that person's spouse in excess of $300,000 in each of those years and has a reasonable expectation of reaching the same income level in the current year.

2. North American Securities Administrators Association, SCOR Statement of Policy (April 28, 1996), www.nasaa.org.

List of International Stock Exchange Web Sites

Americas

American Stock Exchange, United States (www.amex.com/)

Bermuda Stock Exchange, Bermuda (www.bsx.com/)

Buenos Aires Stock Exchange, Argentina (www.bcba.sba.com.ar/ BCBA/)

Columbia Stock Exchange, South America (www.bvc.com.co/ bvcweb/mostrarpagina.jsp)

Lima Stock Exchange, Peru (www.bvl.com.pe/english/)

Mexican Stock Exchange, Mexico (www.bmv.com.mx/)

Montreal Stock Exchange, Canada (www.m-x.ca/accueil_fr.php)

Nasdaq Stock Market, United States (www.nasdaq.com)

New York Stock Exchange, United States (www.nyse.com)

Nicaraguan Stock Exchange, Nicaragua (www.bolsanic.com/)

Rio de Janeiro Stock Exchange, Brazil (www.bvrj.com.br/)

Santiago Stock Exchange, Chili (www.bolsadesantiago.com/)

São Paulo Stock Exchange, Brazil (bovespa.com.br/indexi.asp)

Toronto Stock Exchange, Canada (www.tsx.com/)

Trinidad and Tobago Stock Exchange, Trinidad and Tobago (www.stockex.co.tt/)

Asia Pacific

Australian Stock Exchanges, Australia (www.asx.com.au/)

Bombay Stock Exchange, India (www.bseindia.com/)

Bursa Malaysia (www.bursamalaysia.com/website/bm/)

Columbo Stock Exchange, Columbo (www.cse.lk/welcome.htm)

Hong Kong Exchanges and Clearing Limited, Hong Kong (www.hkex .com.hk/index.htm)

Indonesia NET Exchange, Indonesia (www.indoexchange.com/)

Jasaq Securities Exchange, Japan (www.jasdaq.co.jp/info/info_31 _en.jsp)

Karachi Stock Exchange, Pakistan (www.kse.com.pk/)

Korea Stock Exchange, Korea (www.kse.or.kr/index.html)

National Stock Exchange of India, India (www.nseindia.com/)

New Zealand Stock Exchange, New Zealand (www.nzx.com/)

Osaka Securities Exchange, Japan (www.ose.or.jp/)

Philippine Stock Exchange, Philippines (www.pse.com.ph/)

Shanghai Stock Exchange, China (www.sse.com.cn/sseportal/en_us/ ps/home.shtml)

Shenzhen Stock Exchange, China (www.szse.cn/main/en/)

Singapore Exchange, Singapore (http://www.ses.com.sg/)

Taiwan Stock Exchange, Taiwan (www.tse.com.tw/ch/index.php)

Stock Exchange of Thailand, Thailand (www.set.or.th/th/index.html)

Tokyo Stock Exchange Group, Inc., Japan (www.tse.or.jp/english/ Europe)

Africa—Middle East

Amman Stock Exchange, Jordan (www.ase.com.jo/)

Athens Stock Exchange, Greece (www.ase.gr/)

Barcelona Stock Exchange, Spain (www.borsabcn.es/)

Beirut Stock Exchange, Lebanon (http://www.bse.com.lb/)

Budapest Stock Exchange, Hungary (www.fornax.hu/fmon/stock/betdata.html)

Cairo and Alexandria Stock Exchange, Egypt (www.egyptse.com/main.asp)

Cyprus Stock Exchange, Cyprus (www.cse.com.cy/en/default.asp)

EASDAQ, Belgium (www.equiduct.eu/home/the-group.asp)

Frankfurt Stock Exchange, Germany (www.deutsche-boerse.com/dbag/dispatch/en/kir/gdb_navigation/home)

Irish Stock Exchange, Ireland (www.ise.ie/)

Istanbul Stock Exchange, Turkey (www.ise.org/)

Italian Stock Exchange, Italy (www.borsaitaliana.it/homepage/homepage.htm)

Johannesburg Stock Exchange, South Africa (www.jse.co.za/)

Ljubljana Stock Exchange, Inc., Slovenia (www.ljse.si/html/eng/kazalo.html)

London Stock Exchange (FTSE International), United Kingdom (www.ftse.com/)

Luxembourg Stock Exchange, Luxembourg (http://www.bourse.lu/Accueil.jsp)

Macedonian Stock Exchange, Macedonia (www.mse.org.mk/)

Madrid Stock Exchange, Spain (www.bolsamadrid.es/ing/portada.htm)

Malta Stock Exchange, Malta (www.borzamalta.com.mt/)

The Stock Exchange of Maritius, Republic of Maritius (www.semdex.com/contact.htm)

OMX Nordic Exchange, Norway (www.omxnordicexchange.com/)

Oslo Bors Stock Exchange (www.oslobors.no/ob/?languageID=1)

Paris Stock Exchange, France (www.euronext.com/index-2166-FR.htmlbourse/sbf/homesbf-gb.htlm)

Swiss Exchange, Switzerland (www.swx.com/index.html)

Tehran Stock Exchange, Iran (www.iranbourse.com/Default.aspx?tabid=36)

Tel Aviv Stock Exchange, Israel (www.tase.co.il/tase/)

Warsaw Stock Exchange, Poland (www.gpw.pl/index.asp)

Wiener Börse Stock Exchange, Vienna (http://en.wienerborse.at/)

Zagreb Stock Exchange, Croatia (www.zse.hr/)

Responses of International Exchanges to IPO Survey

TORONTO STOCK EXCHANGE (CANADA) (TSX)

Question: What do you view as the primary advantage or advantages of a listing on your stock exchange in connection with an IPO?

Answer:

Advantages of IPO on Toronto Stock Exchange

Dual exchange structure (senior board: Toronto Stock Exchange; junior board: TSX Venture Exchange) to support broader range of companies from early stage, development companies though to global players.

With almost 4000 listed companies, TSX Group has companies from microcap to megacap, but particular strength in supporting companies in the U.S. $100 million to U.S. $500 million market cap range, which are not currently supported by the U.S. capital markets.

Analyst coverage at a far earlier stage for a company on TSX Group than could be seen with a U.S. listing at an equivalent stage.

World's seventh largest equity marketplace, with participants from around the world.

Access to North American capital, supported by global investors.

World's largest exchange for the listing and financing of mining-related companies.

World's largest exchange for oil and gas listed companies.

World's second largest exchange for technology and life science companies.

Question: What do you view as the primary disadvantage or disadvantages of a listing on your stock exchange in connection with an IPO?

Answer:

Disadvantages of IPO on Toronto Stock Exchange Group

Smaller pool of retail and institutional investors, compared to U.S. market, if company seeks to target only Canadian investors.

Depending on sector and company story, there may be a slight valuation discount if company is seeking only a Canadian financing as opposed to a full North American financing.

Question: Does your stock exchange permit so-called short-selling?

Answer:

Short Selling

Yes, under the guidelines set by the Universal Market Integrity Rules, as mandated by Market Regulations Services Inc.

OMX NORDIC EXCHANGE (NORWAY)

PROS AND CONS OF LISTING AT OMX NORDIC EXCHANGE[1]

Question: What do you view as the primary advantage or advantages of a listing on your stock exchange in connection with an IPO?

Answer:

OMX Nordic Exchange operates 365 days a year and is a world leading partner in more than 50 countries. With more efficient securities transactions, OMX is a part of every link in the transaction chain, owning and operating exchanges as well as providing world-leading transaction technology.

OMX Nordic Exchange has existed since the nineteenth century and over time has gained great knowledge and experience of the market.

One of the most common reasons for going public is to raise capital. The Nordic Exchange provides you with a large, attractive home market and considerable pool of capital. We have today 853 listed companies[2] and a market cap of EUR 804 billion.[3]

Once a company is listed, there are many aspects that will change. One important thing that will change is visibility (increased media attention), and to emphasize this we use products and services such as webcasts, liquidity provider, IR modules, news distribution service, Nordic investment meeting, and distribution of annual reports. Going public will also open up doors for a global investment community and a strong retail investor segment.

With our Global Industry Classification Standard (GICS), which divides the companies into 10 sectors and segments division (which divides the companies into three segments: Large Cap, Mid Cap, and Small Cap, depending on market capitalization), it is much easier to compare companies with each other both on OMX Nordic Exchange as well as with companies on other exchanges.

Being listed on the Nordic Exchange will be seen as a quality stamp and the company will be viewed as a successful company. The surveillance department makes sure that all the rules and regulations are followed and therefore serves as a safety net.

Although the market is currently a bit uncertain, the Nordic Exchange is able to maintain liquidity, stay efficient, and remain as a quality exchange that is highly ranked in Europe and Internationally. We have a large number of trading members and real-time information vendors, a high turnover velocity rate compared to other exchanges, and a very strong retail market.

The statistics for 2007 show records on many levels such as turn-over and number of trades.

Highlights 2007

- The total share trading (including over-the-counter [OTC] trades) in 2007 amounted to SEK 12,179 billion, corresponding to an average daily turnover of SEK 48,743 million, thus making 2007 the best year ever in terms of trading (2006: SEK 38,865 million per day).

- The number of trades per day (including OTC trades) also reached an all time high, with 191,057 trades per day during 2007 (2006: 124,480 trades per day).

- The derivatives trading on OMX Nordic Exchange in 2007 amounted to 658,314 contracts per day, which is the best year ever (2006: 601,514 contracts per day).

With five turnover records and three records for number of trades set in share trading during 2007, we have both managed to handle the peaks and the structural growth in trading. The inflow of new investment op-portunities has continued from last year giving us 93 new companies and we are especially pleased with the interest outside the Nordics for listing on the Nordic Exchange. For 2008 we have already announced a number of initiatives, like fee cuts and post anonymity trading, in order to further enhance the new trading behaviors that are becoming more and more dominant on the European exchanges.[4]

Question: What do you view as the primary disadvantage or disadvan-tages of a listing on your stock exchange in connection with an IPO?

Answer: Not much negatives but consequences. Being in the public eye a company will be monitored both closely and critically by in-vestors, business partners, media, and competitors among others to a far greater extent than before. This is not always a positive thing—comments from management can be misjudged and by being public, this misjudgment can lead to unfortunate consequen-ces for the company; the media can make exaggerations of statements made by the company, make statements that are not always true, etc.

Not all companies are suited/ready for going public, which can lead to substantial consequences.

Question: Does your stock exchange permit so-called short-selling?
Answer: Yes.

TEL AVIV STOCK EXCHANGE (ISRAEL)

Question: What do you view as the primary advantage or advantages of a listing on your stock exchange in connection with an IPO?
Answer: Listing on the Tel Aviv Stock Exchange (TASE) is a good opportunity for foreign companies from all over the globe. Beginning with the Israeli equity market, which is active, advanced, innovative, and creative, initial public offerings on the TASE have more advantages:

- Being a "big fish in a small lake." The Israeli stock market ensures global company prominence and high visibility.
- The dual-listing possibility offers companies traded in the United States and United Kingdom an attractive way to dual-list their shares on the TASE and enjoy many advantages.
- A company listed on the TASE can easily be dual-listed on New York and London markets, and then report only according to U.S. or U.K. regulations to both exchanges it is listed on (TASE and LSE; TASE and Nasdaq; TASE and NYSE).
- The Israel capital market enables the companies to issue limited budget convertible bonds/notes or warrants and not only shares. This expands the financing and capital-raising possibilities.
- Listing on TASE gives the company the ability to be part of the TASE's successful and varied indices and active index products market.

Exhibit B.1 IPO Costs for a U.S. $50 Million Offering ($K)

	United States	United Kingdom	Israel
Fixed costs	1,475	1,365	155
Variable costs	3,500	2,500	2,500
Total	**4,975**	**3,865**	**2,655**

Exhibit B.2 Annual Maintenance Costs ($K)

	United States	United Kingdom	Israel
General costs	1,800	822	260
Directors' and officers' insurance	250	50–60	20
Class actions (estimate)	250	–	–
Total	**2,300** ~	**900** ~	**280**

Source: Canaccord Adams, June 2006.

- Low costs for an IPO, and even more important, low maintenance cost (see Exhibits B.1 and B.2).
- Fixed costs include lawyers, certified public accountants (CPAs), printing, fees, public relations (PR), and the like.
- Variable costs include underwriting and distribution.
- General costs include: lawyers, CPAs, IR, PR [public relations], fees, shareholders meetings, payments and options for directors.

More information regarding IPOs and listing on TASE can be found on our Web site: www.tase.co.il.

Question: What do you view as the primary disadvantage or disadvantages of a listing on your stock exchange in connection with an IPO?

Answer: No response.

Question: Does your stock exchange permit so-called short-selling?

Answer: Full information regarding short selling can be found on our Web site, in the following link: www.tase.co.il/TASEEng/TradingandClearing/Trading/Short+Sale/.

NOTES

1. *Source:* OMX Monthly Statistics Report, December 2007.
2. Including our growth market, First North, which today has 127 listed companies.
3. Including our growth market, First North, which today has a market cap of 5.3 billion euros.
4. Statement from Jukka Ruuska, president, Nordic Marketplaces OMX.

Index